COMING UP D.C.

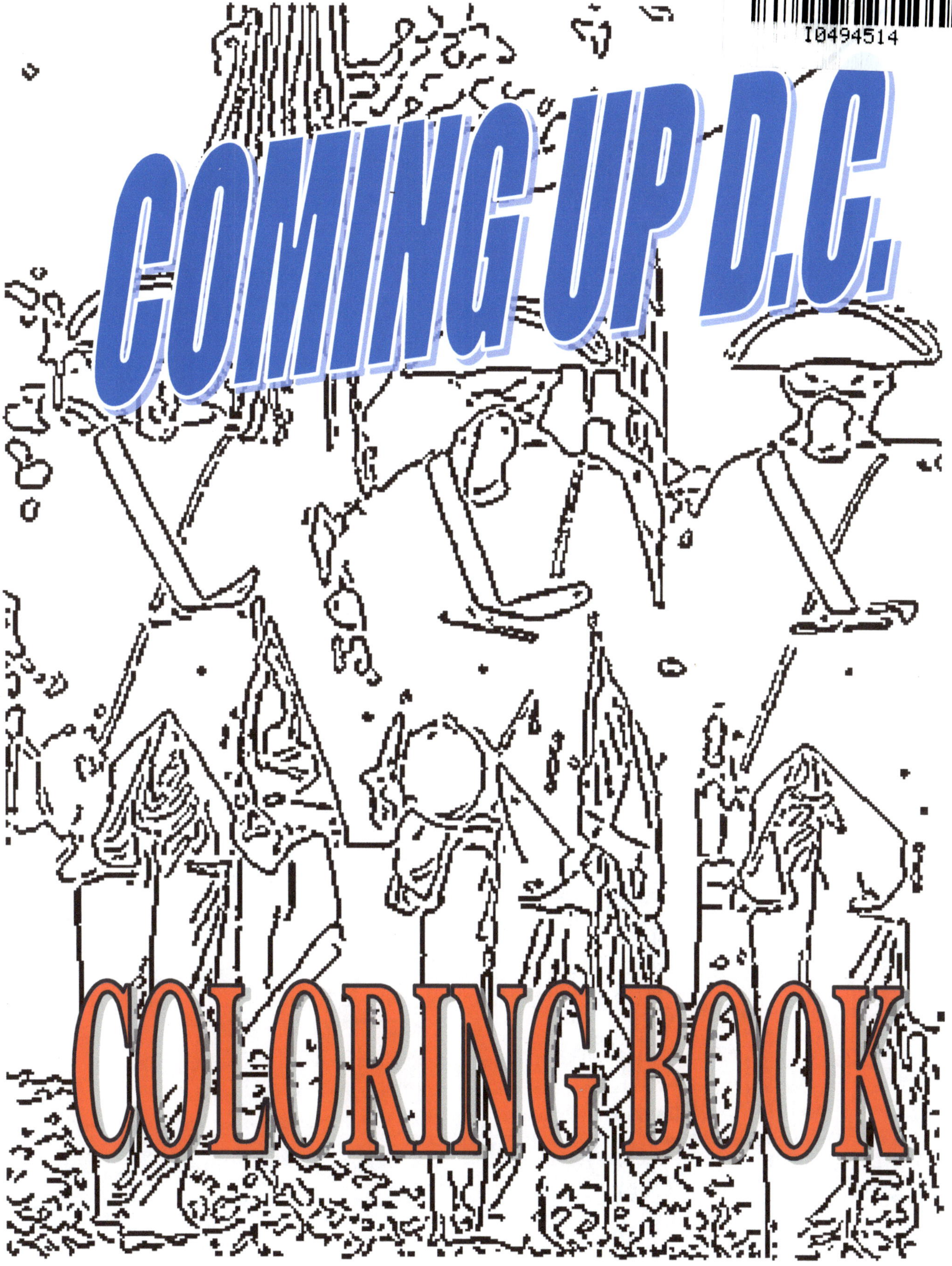

COLORING BOOK

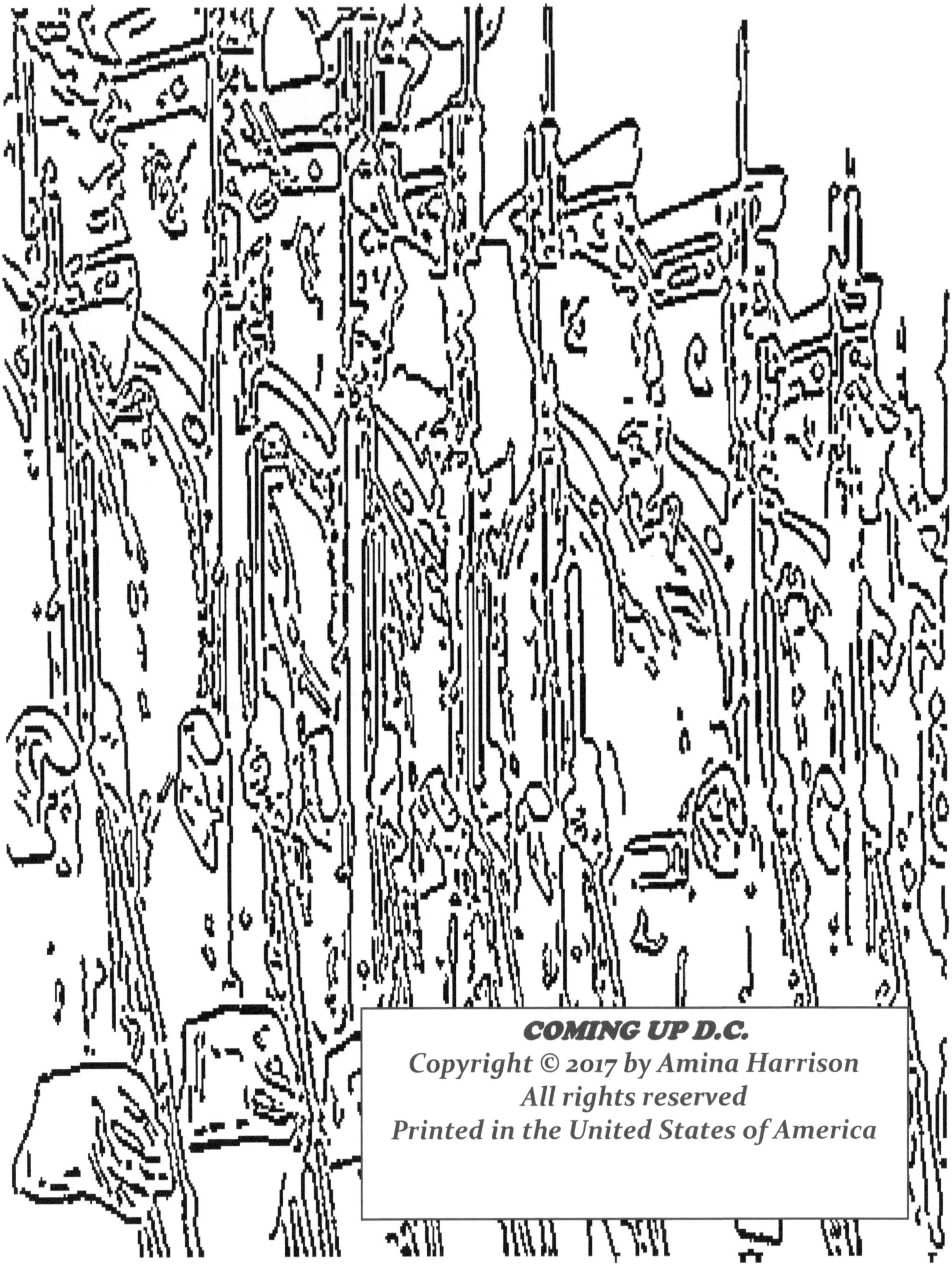

COMING UP D.C.

Printed in the United States of America

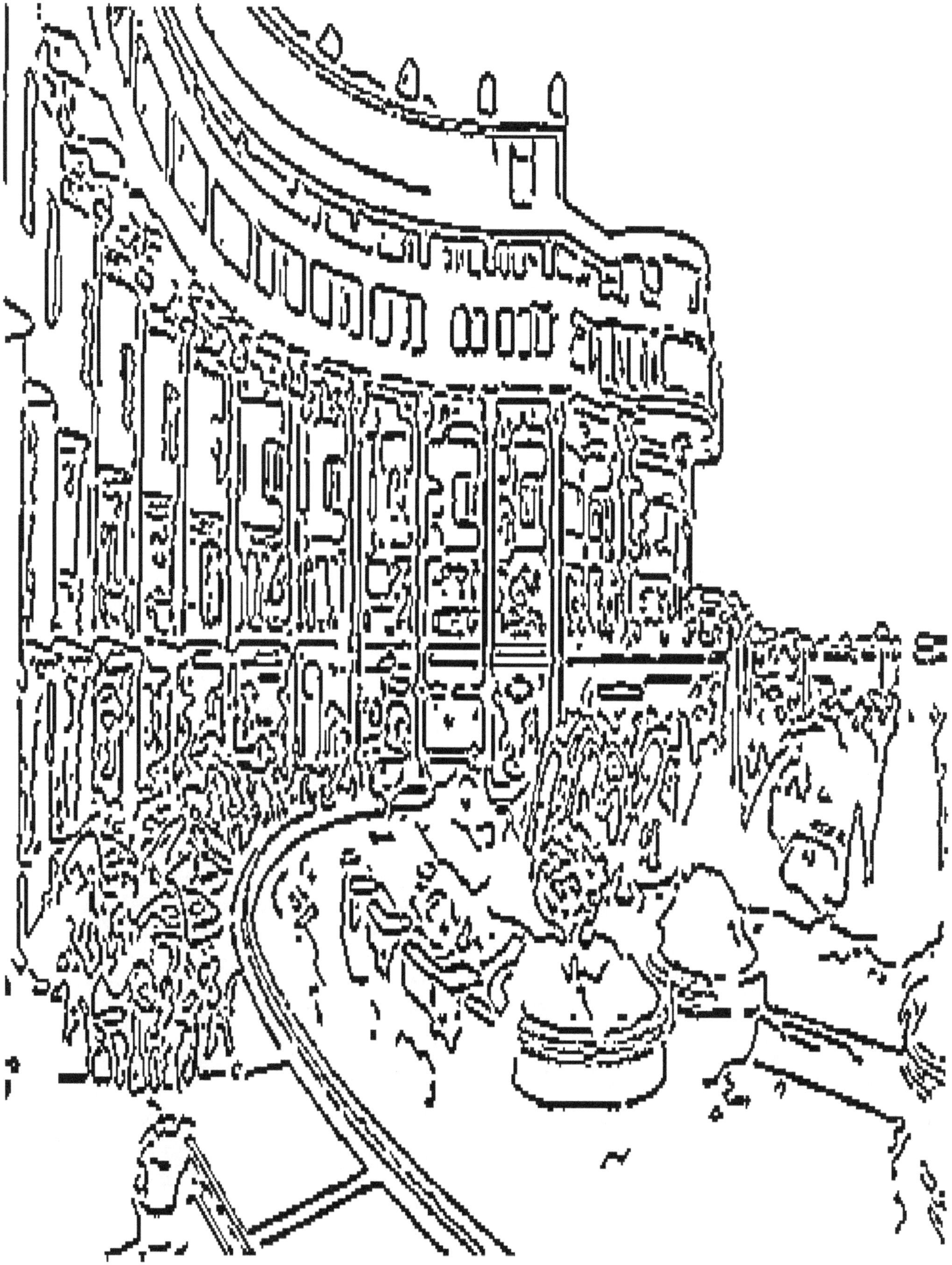

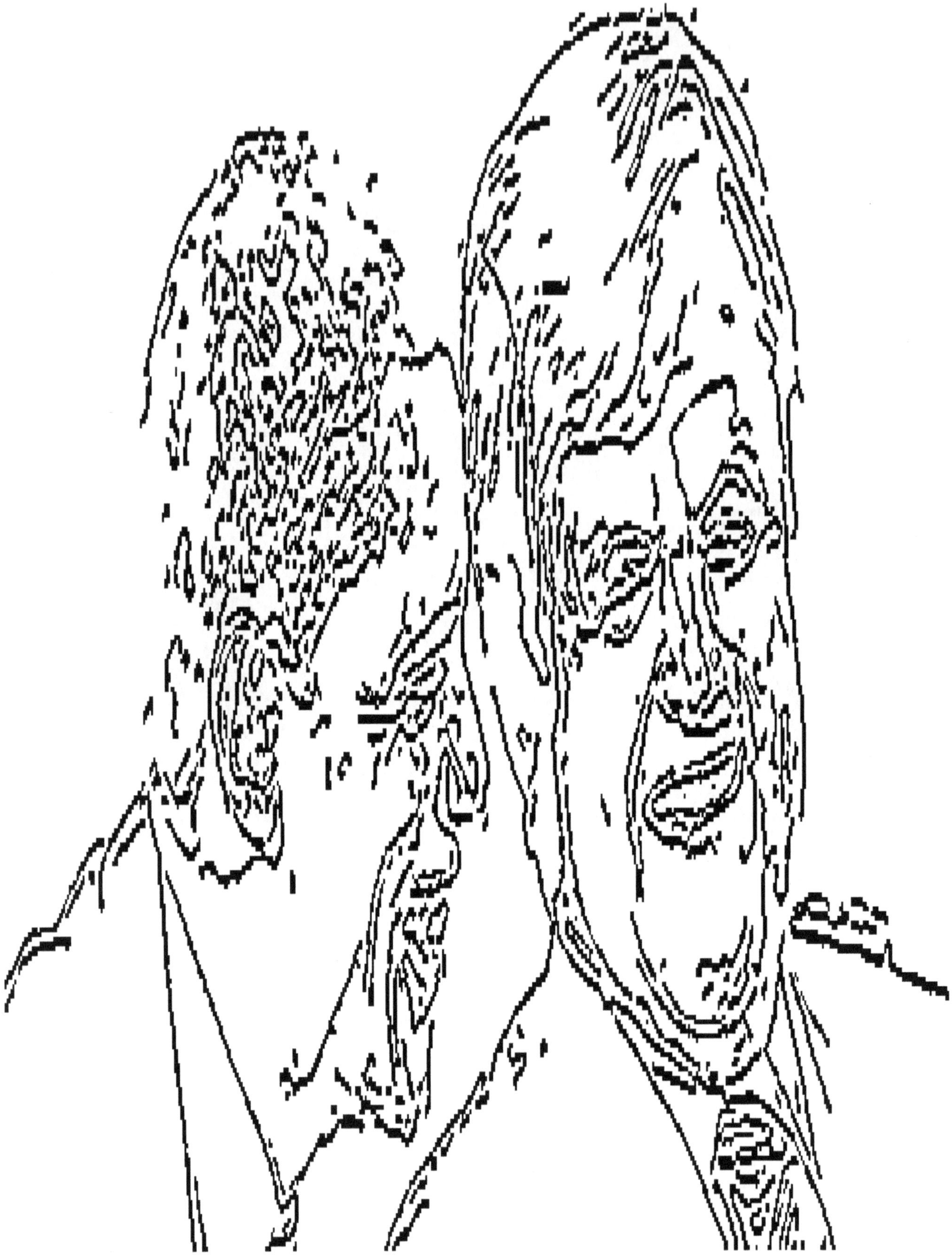

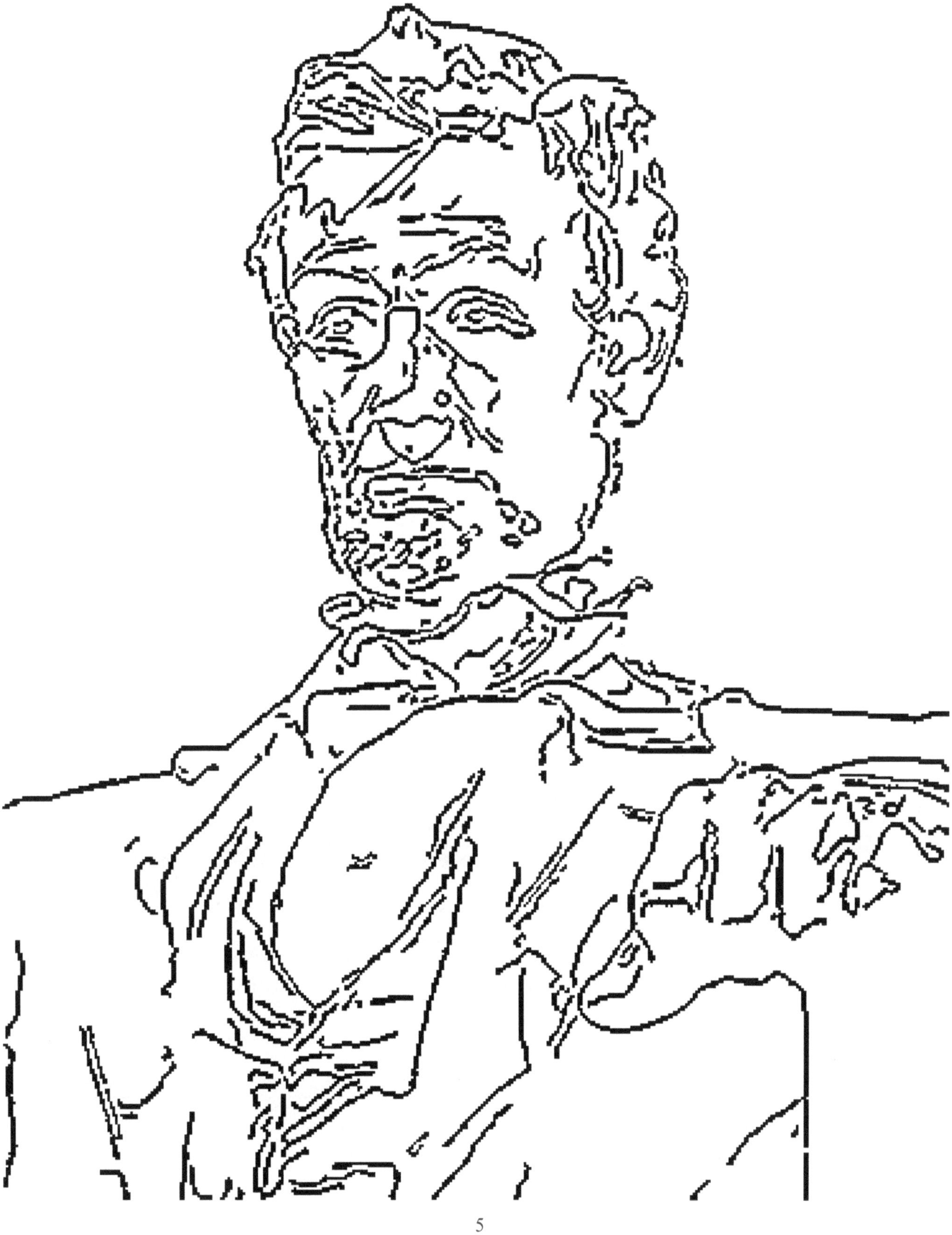

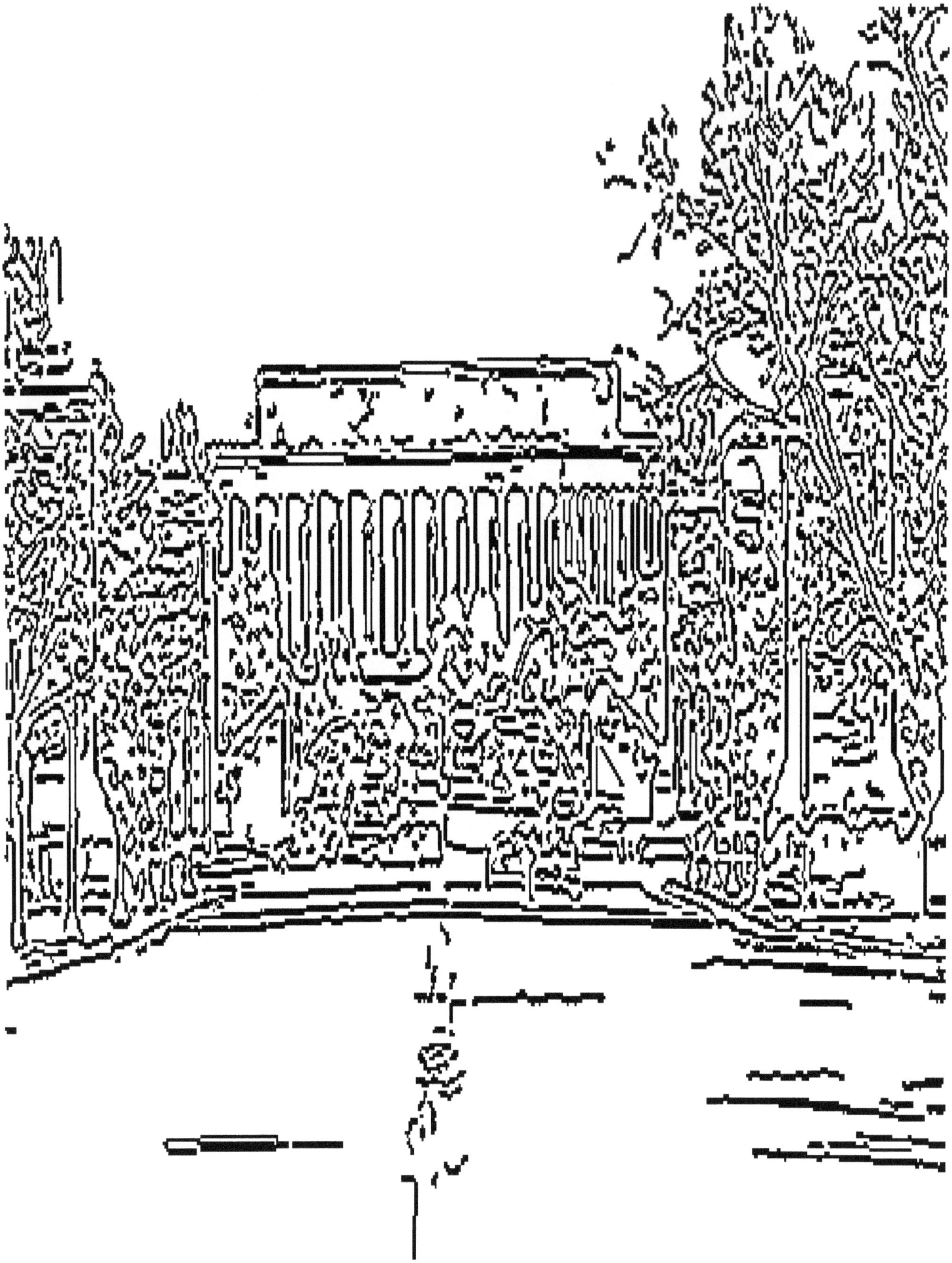

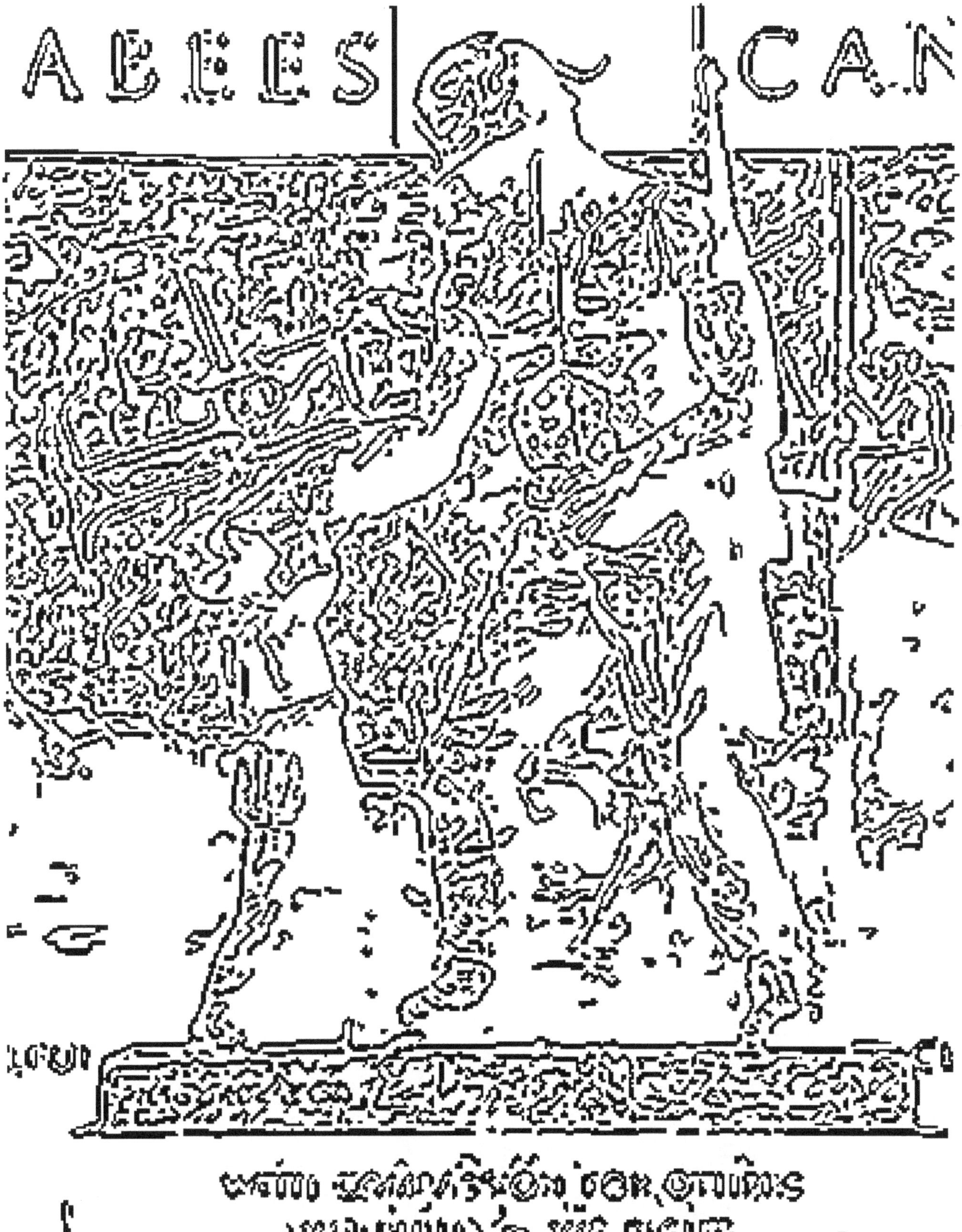
ABEES
CAN

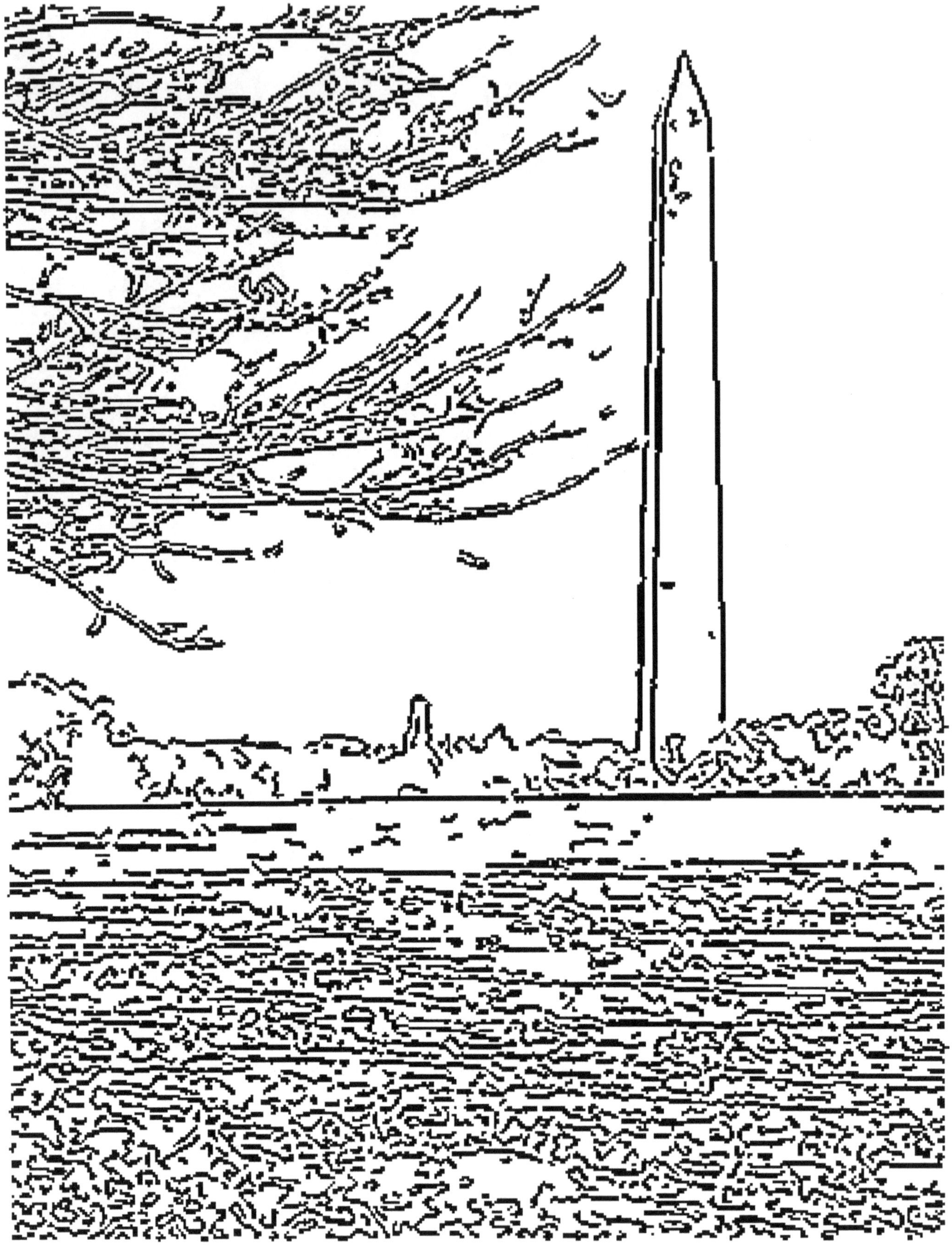

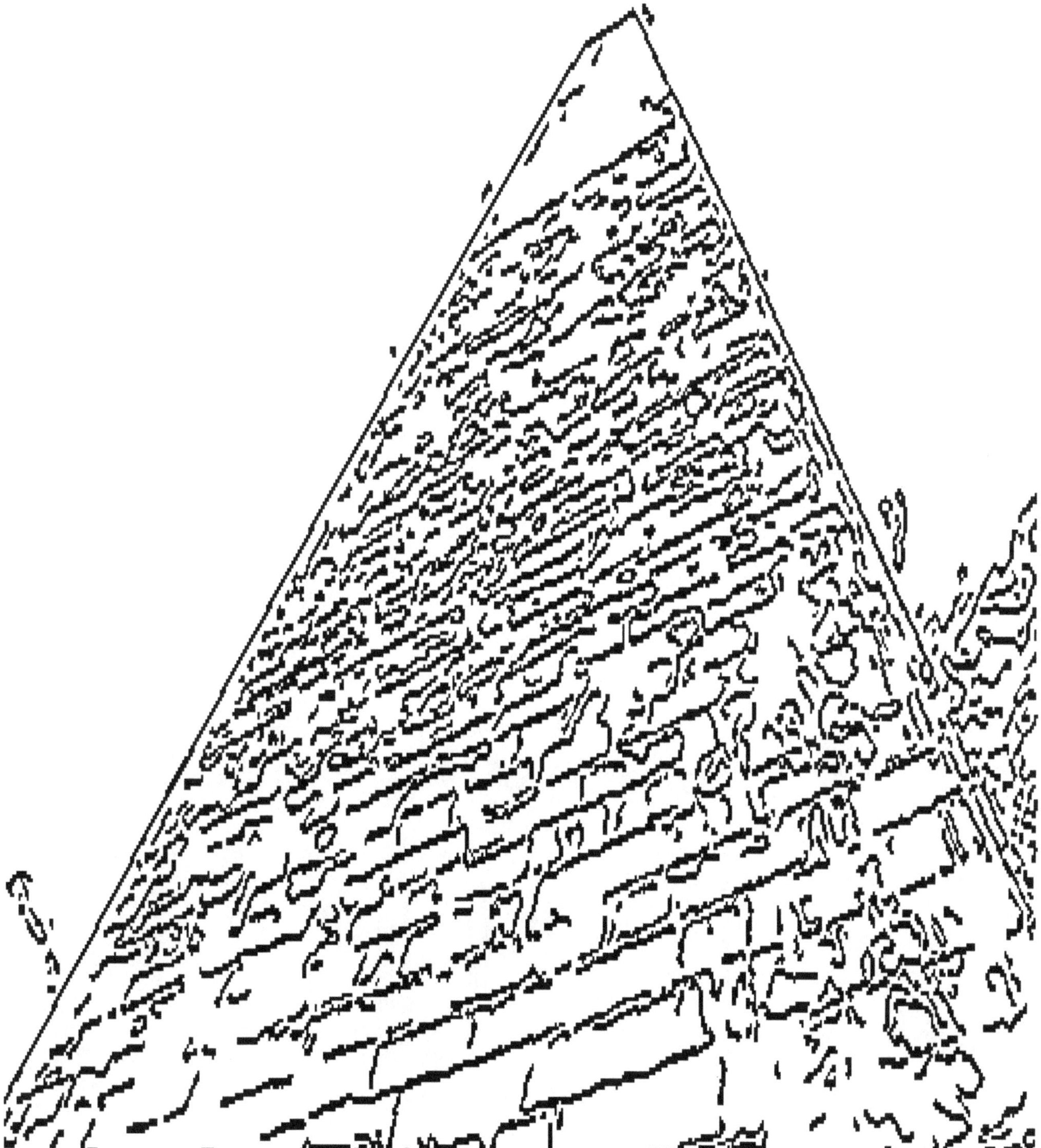

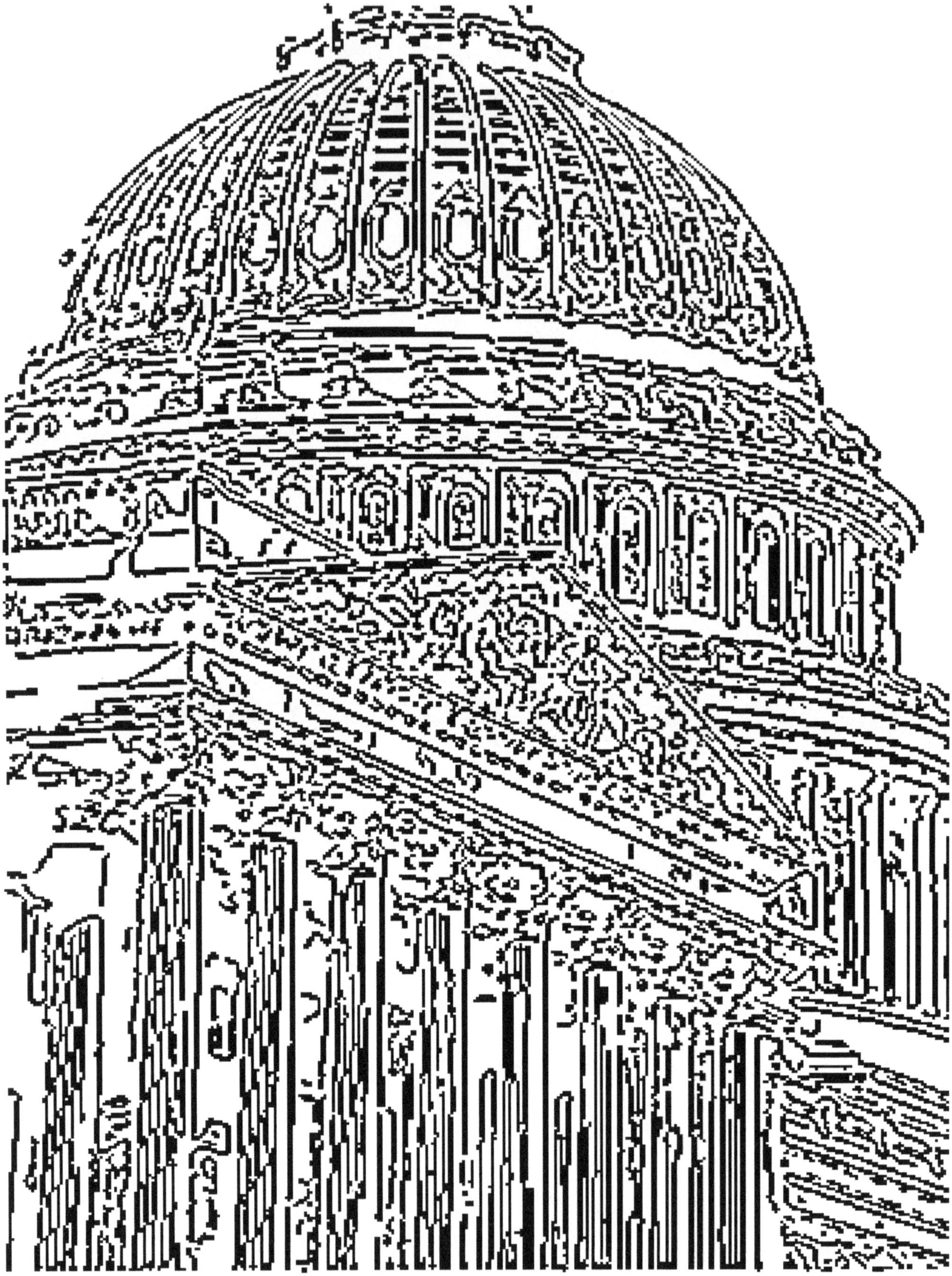

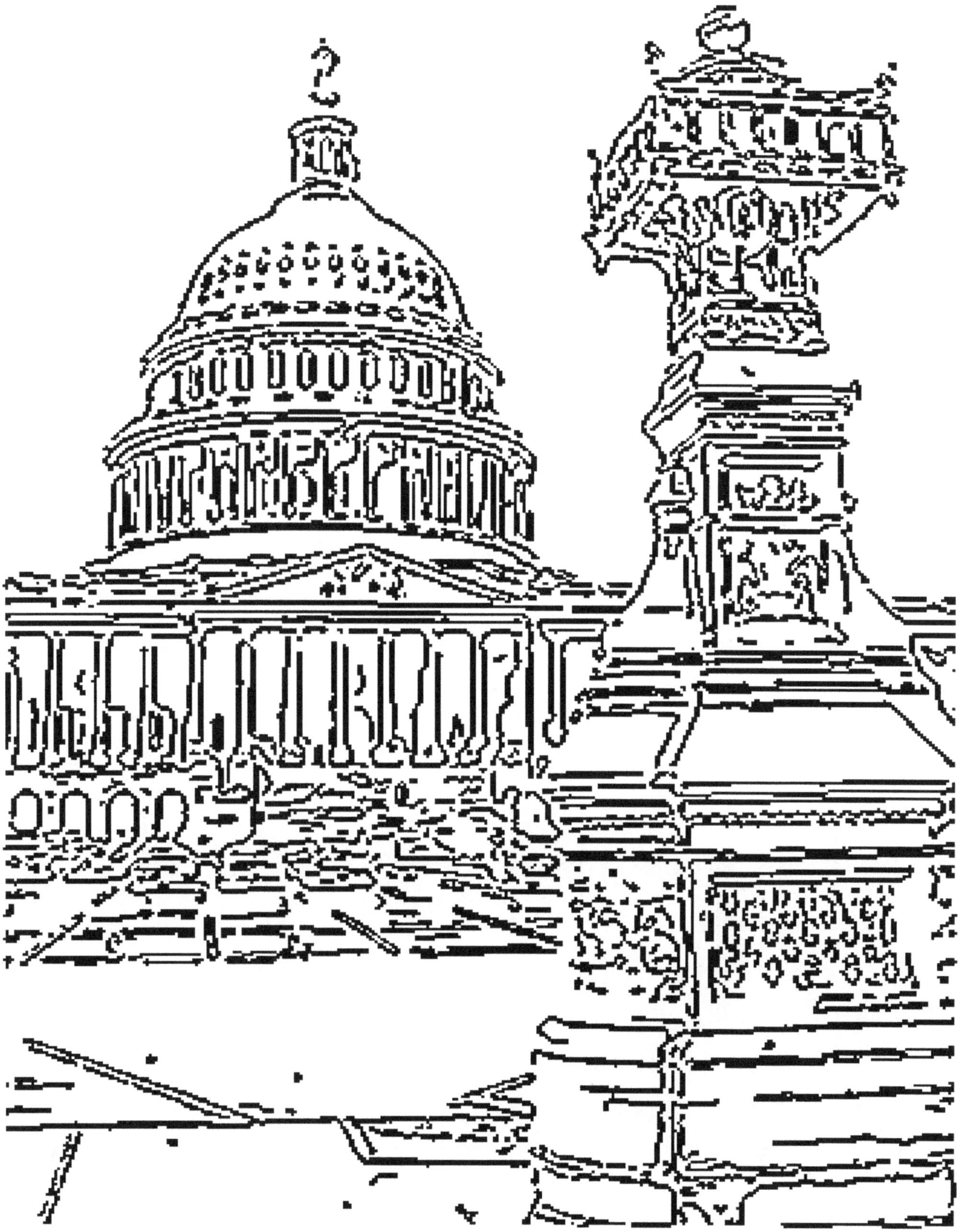

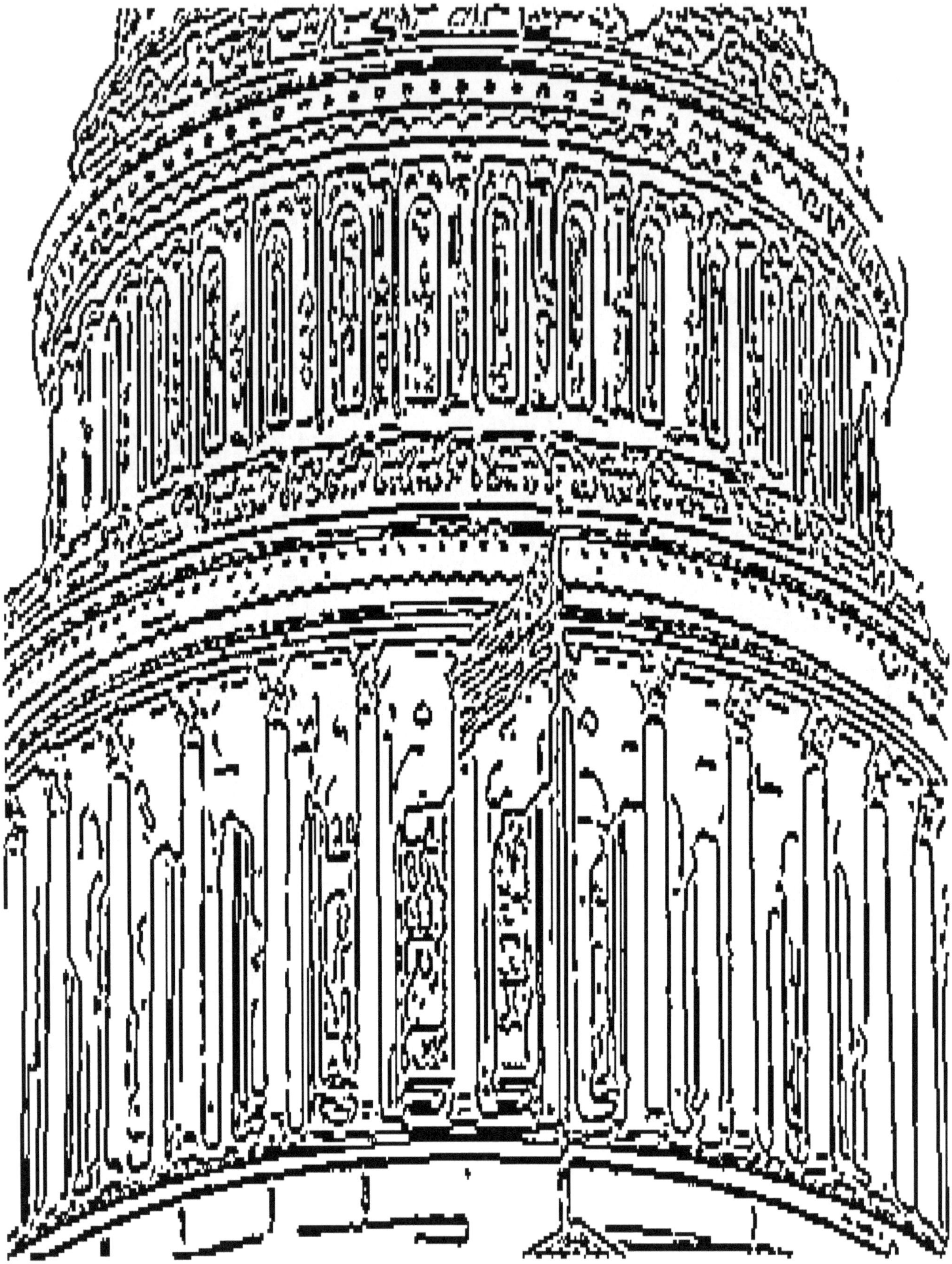

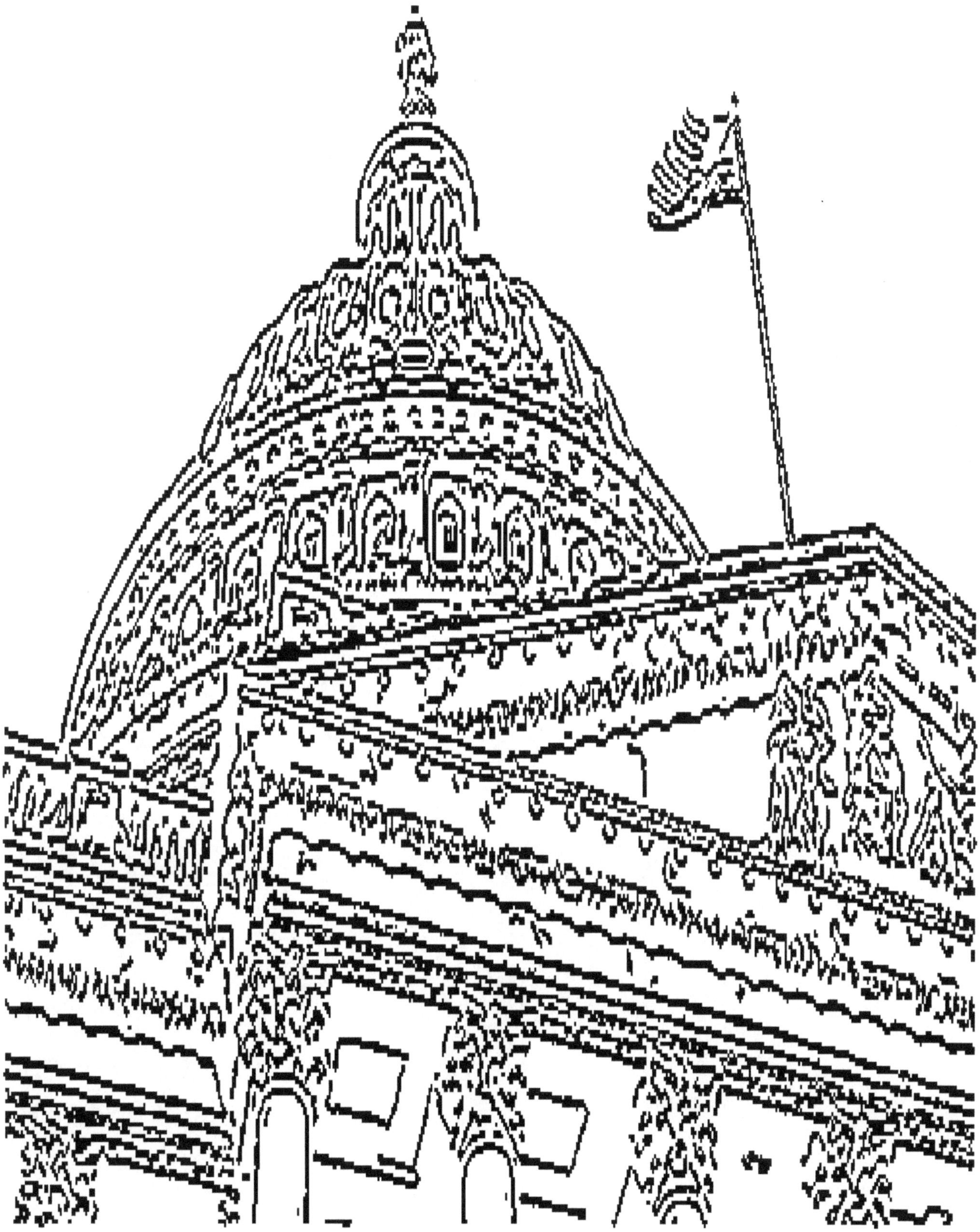

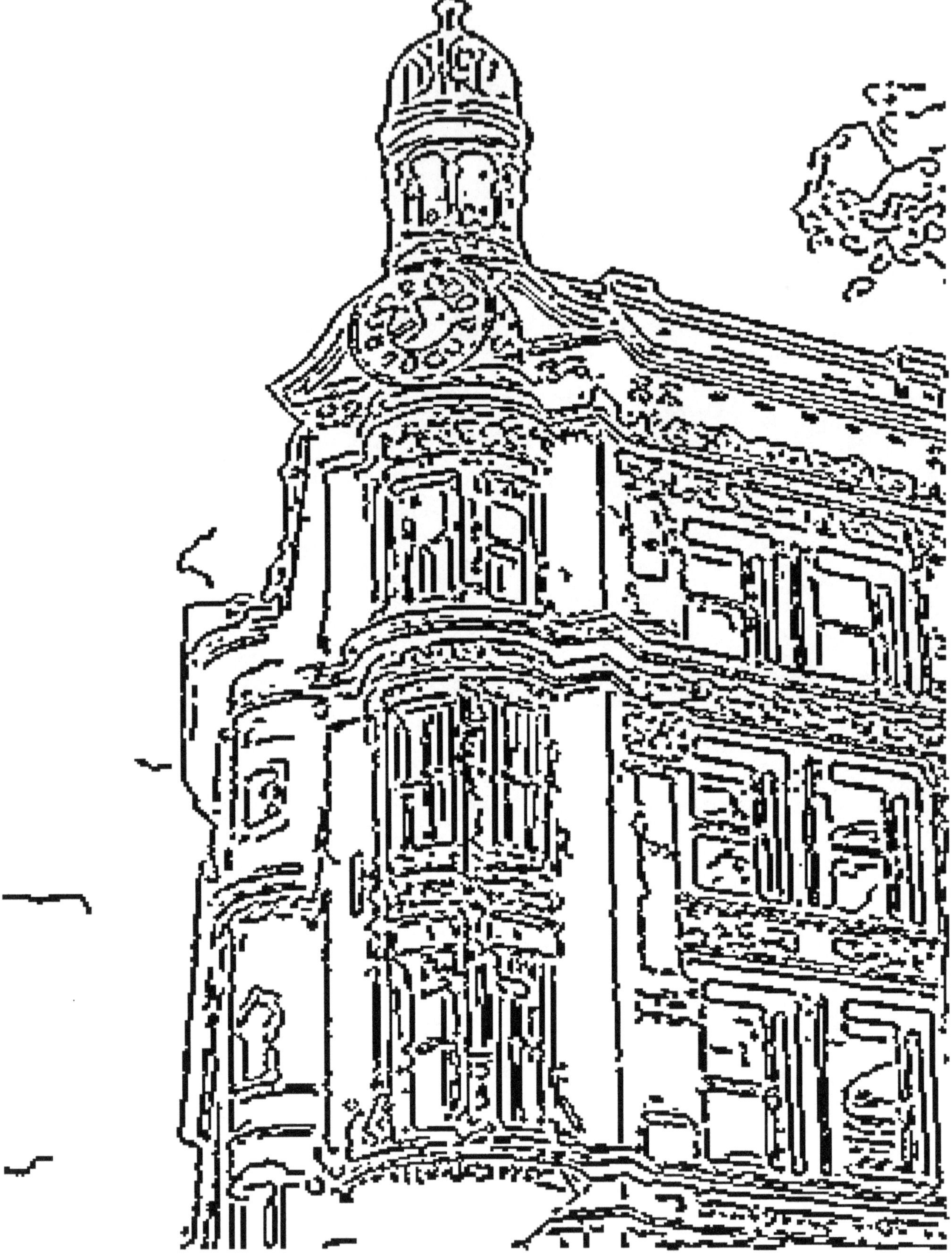

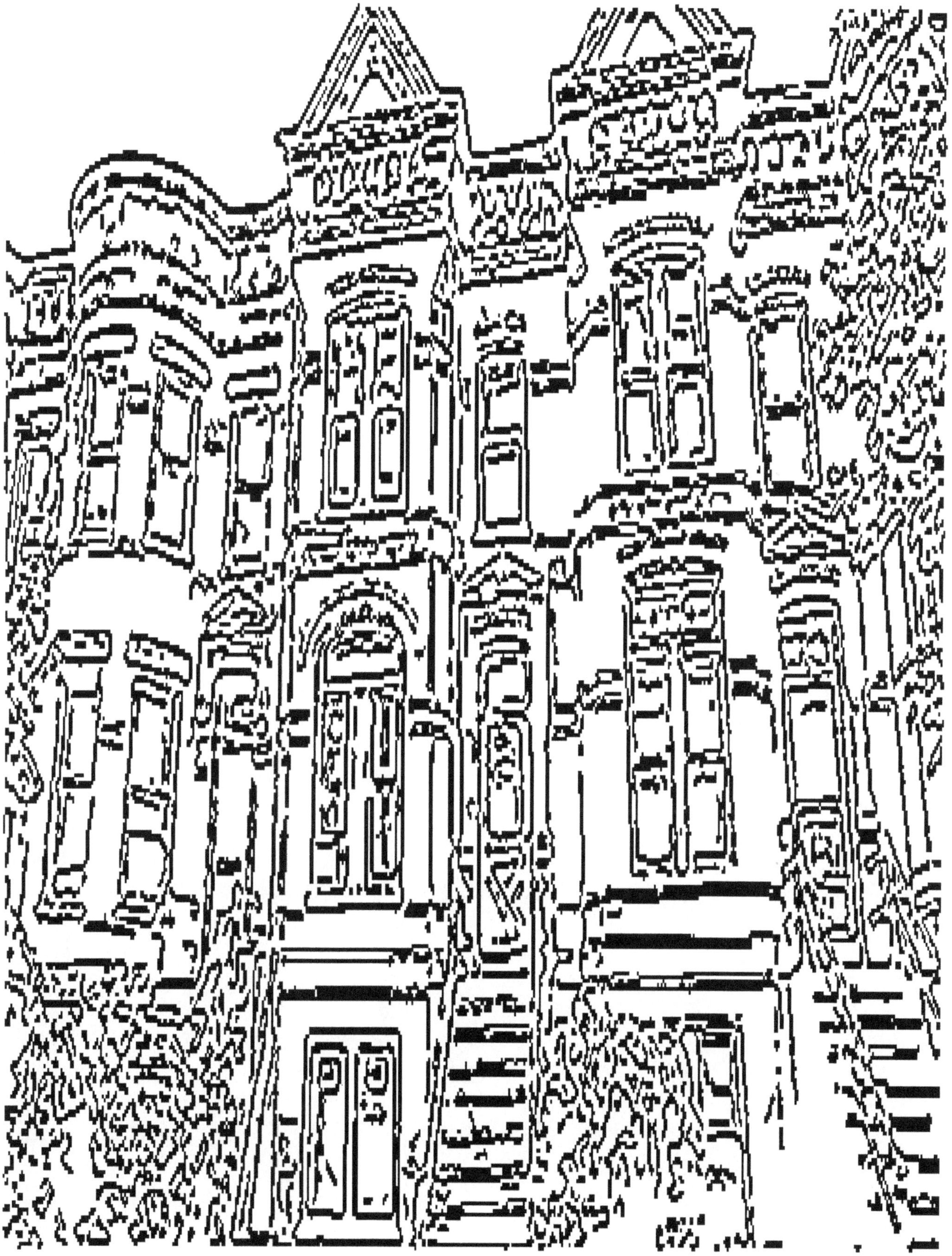

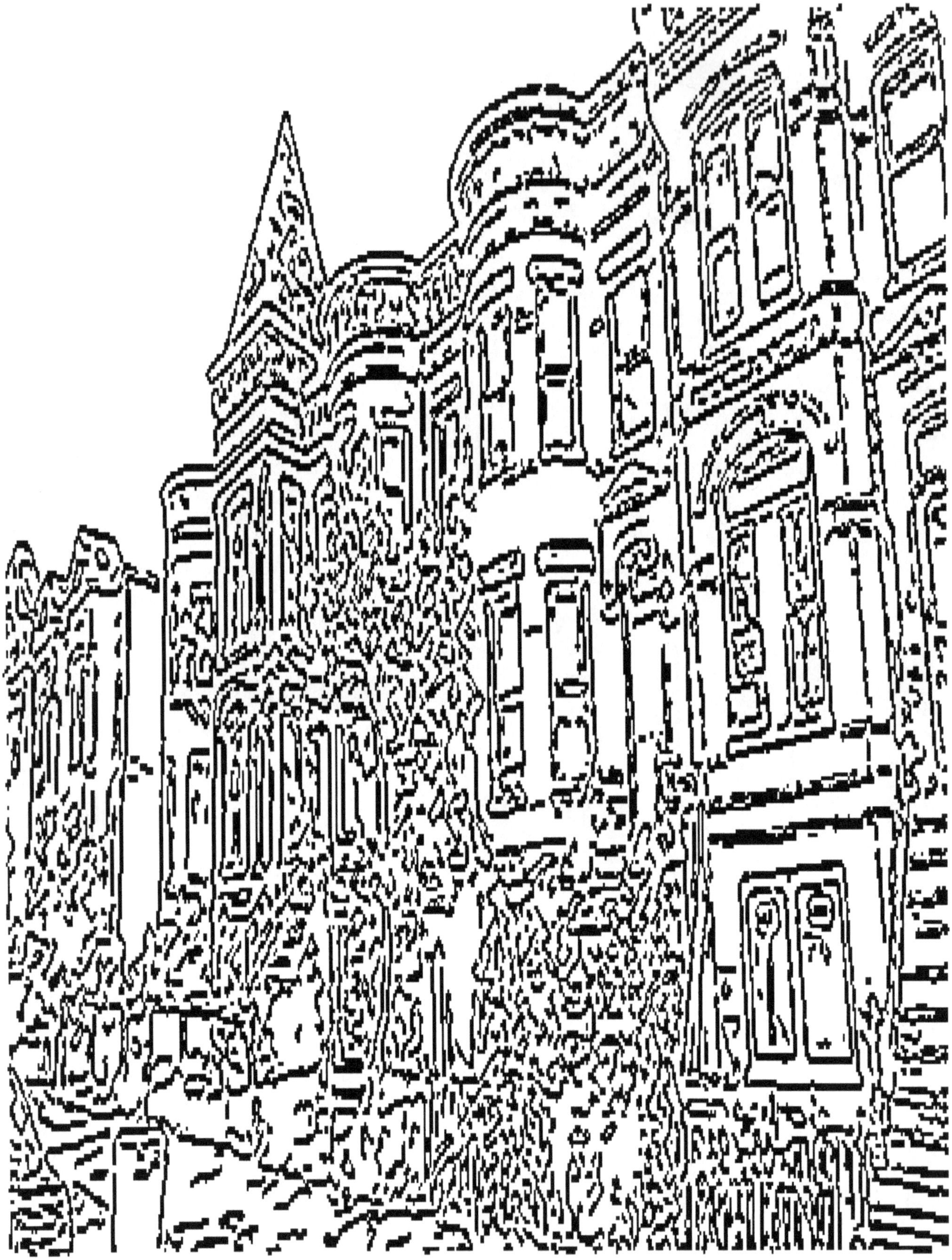

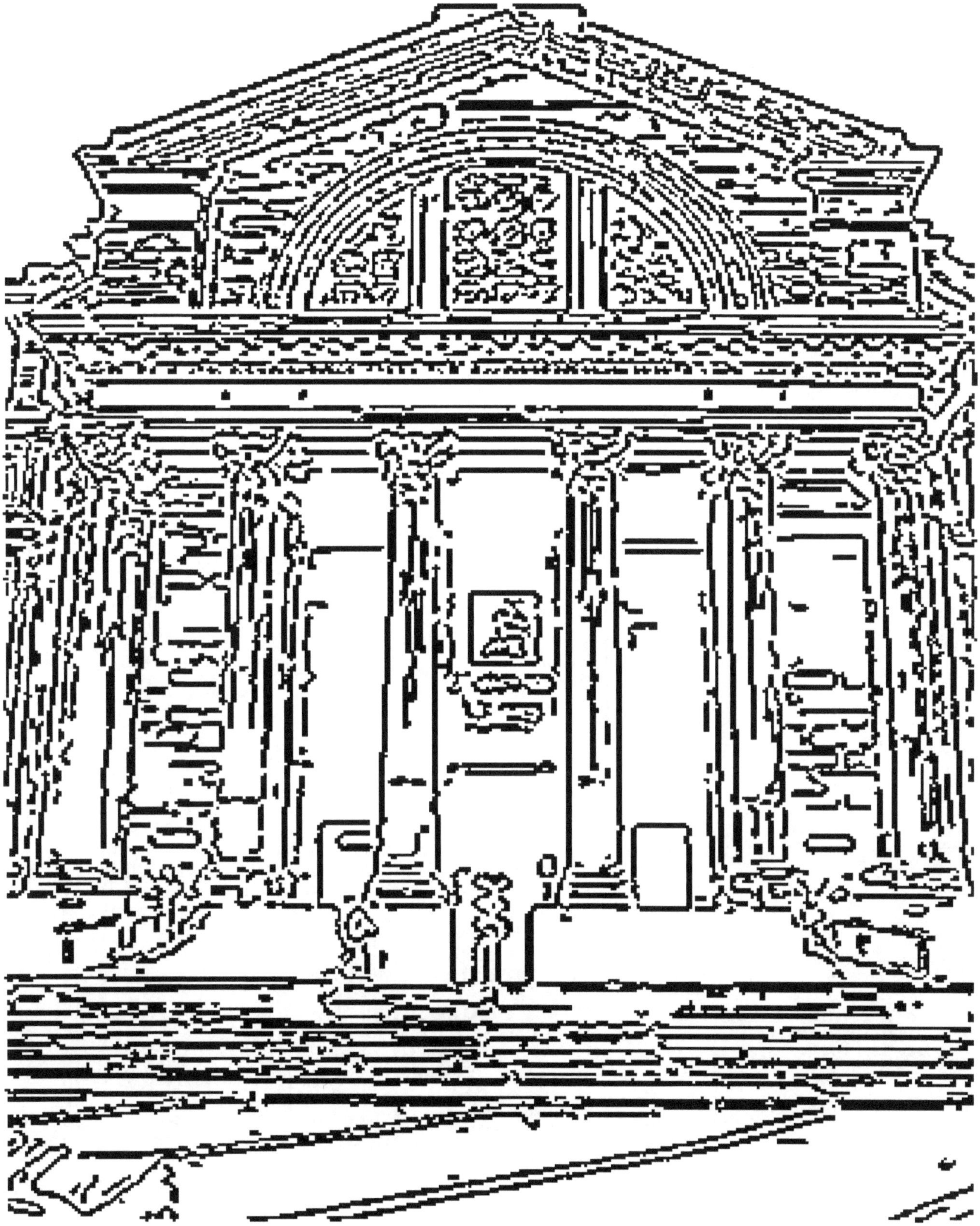

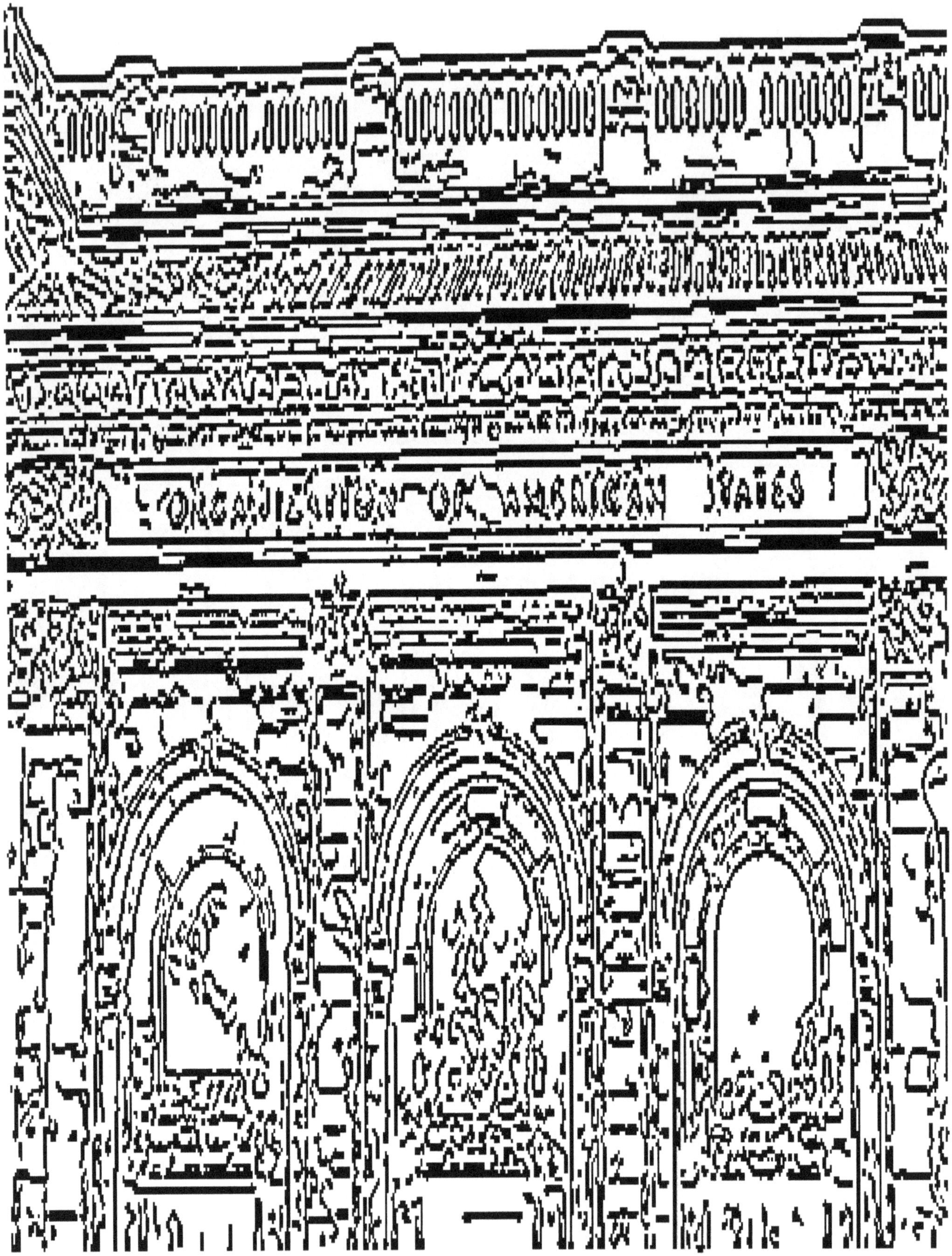
ORGANIZATION OF AMERICAN STATES

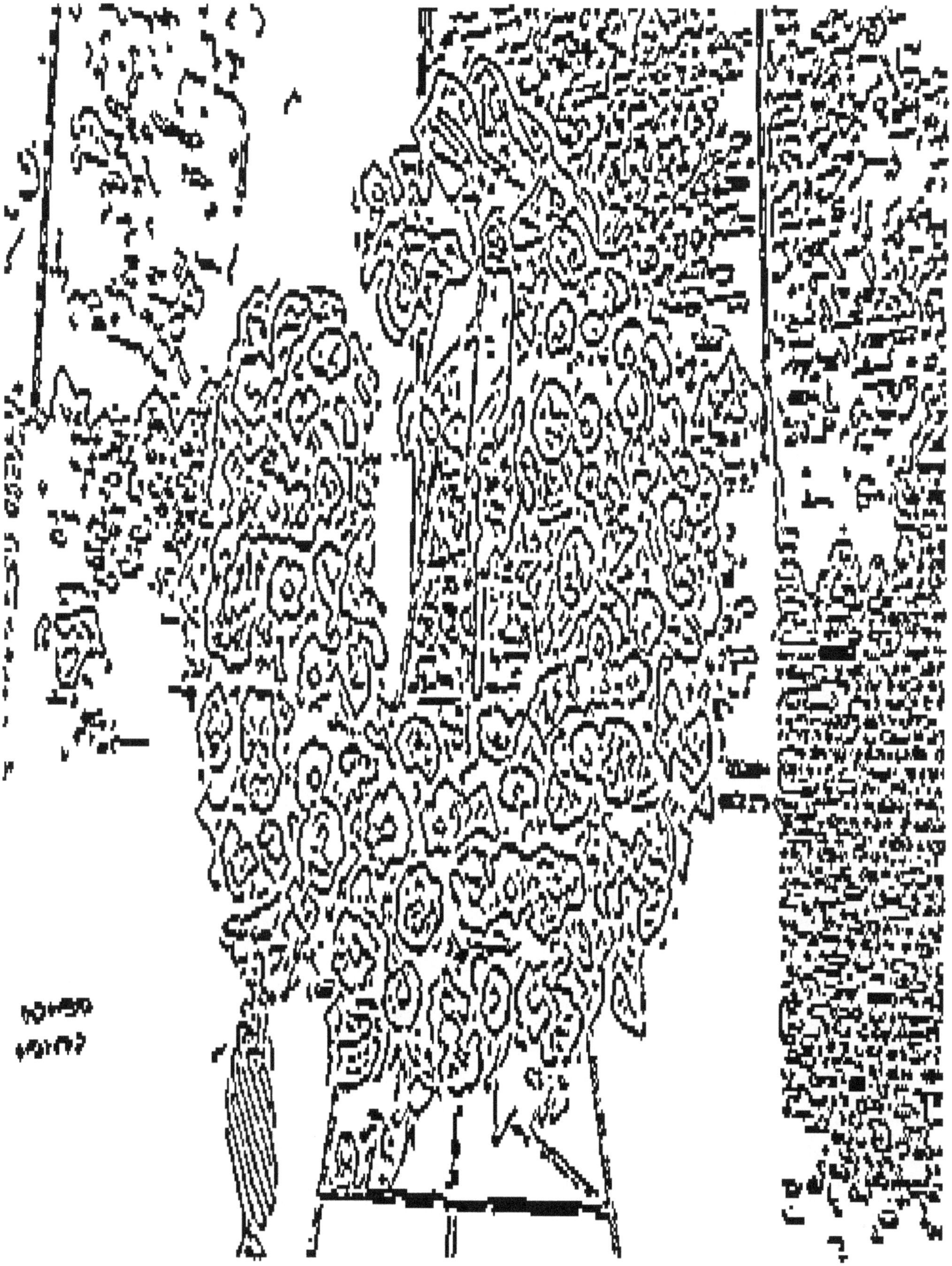

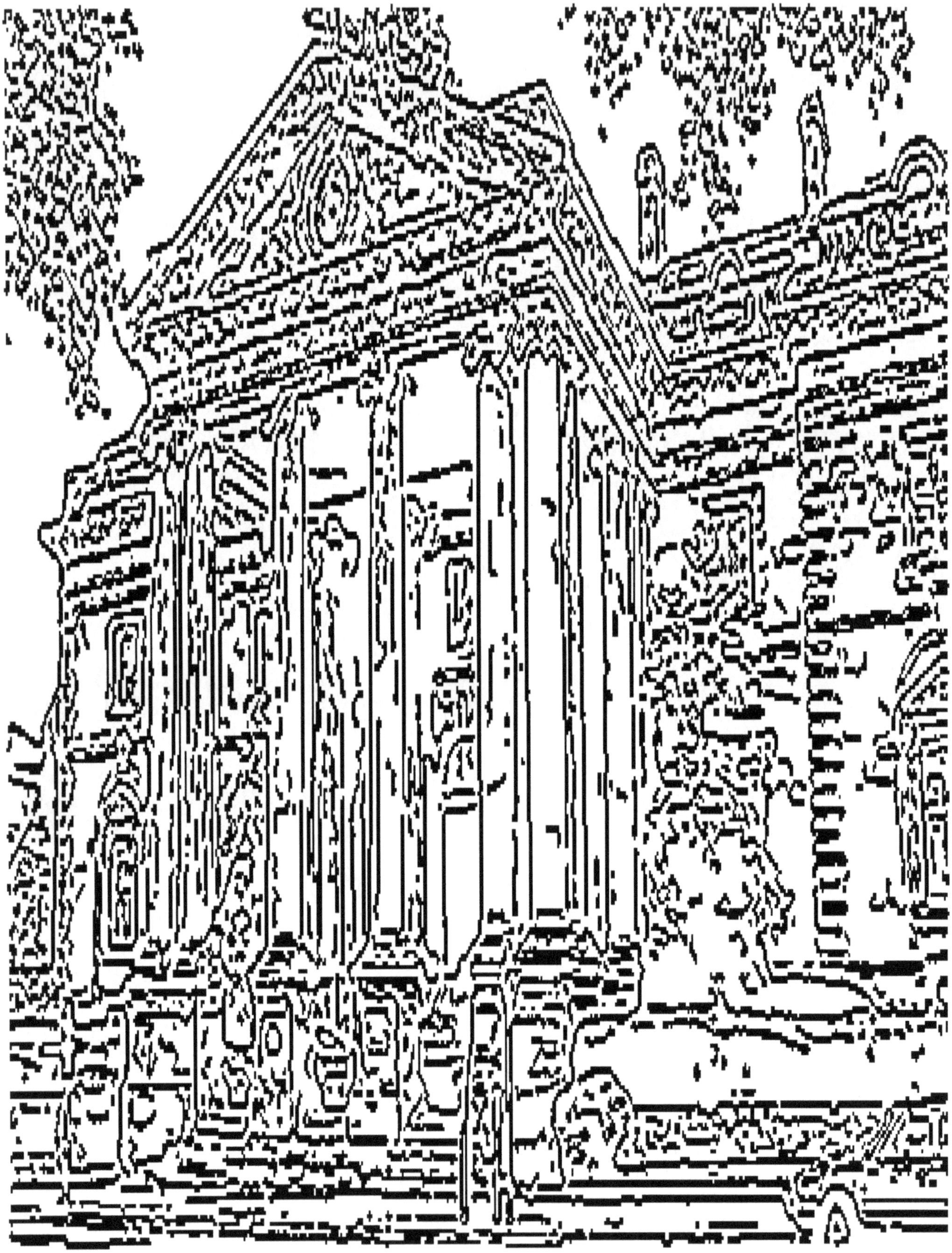

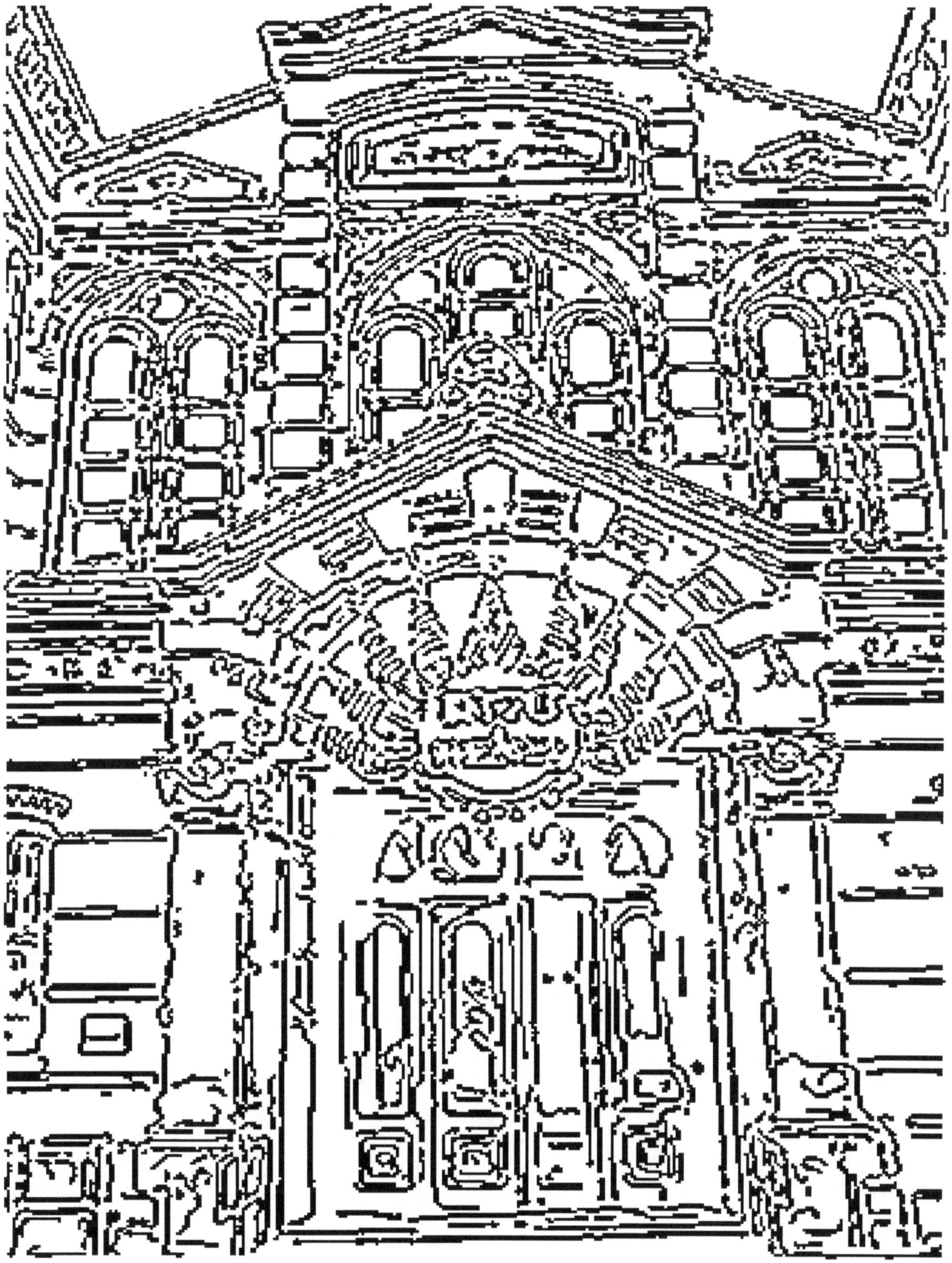

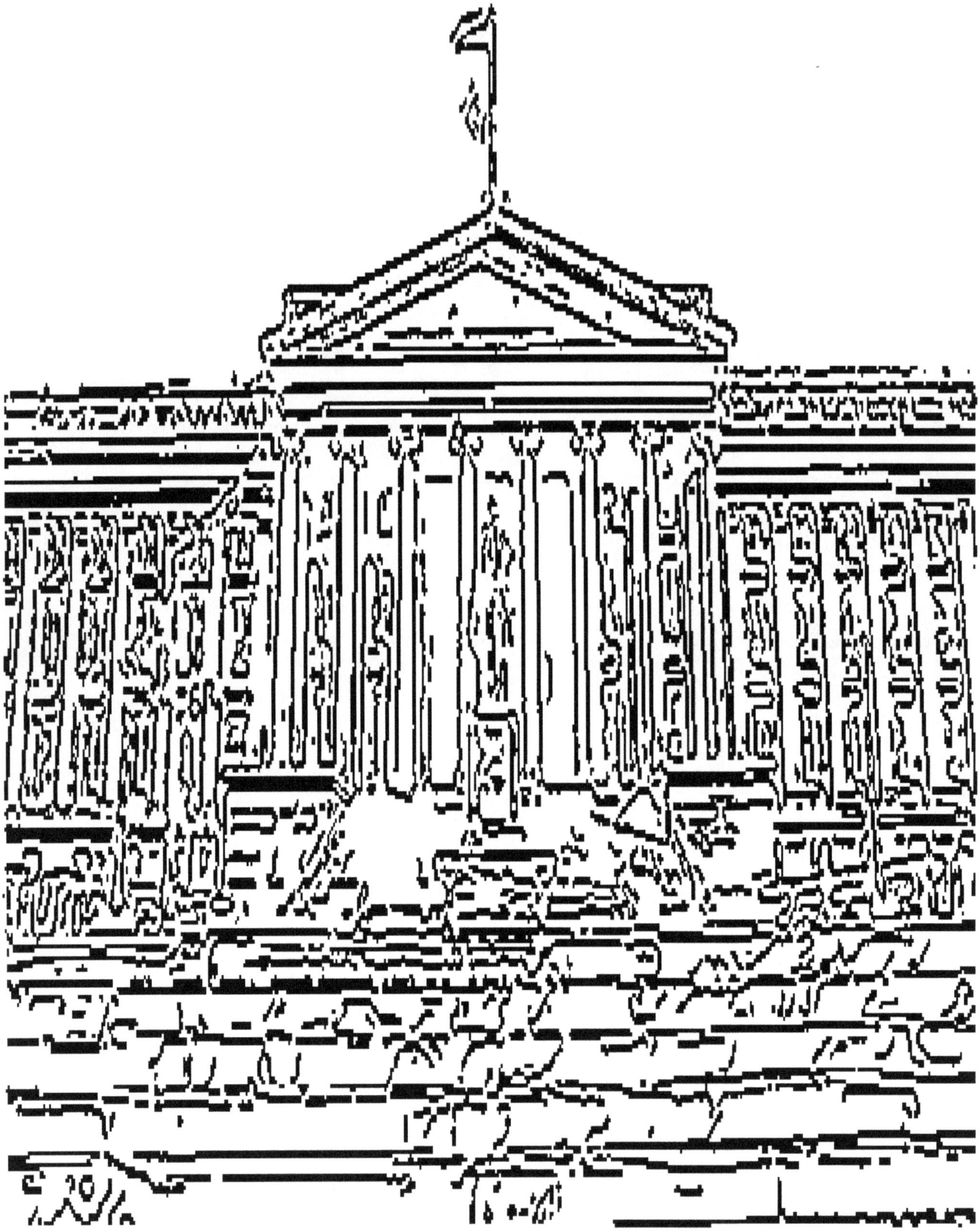

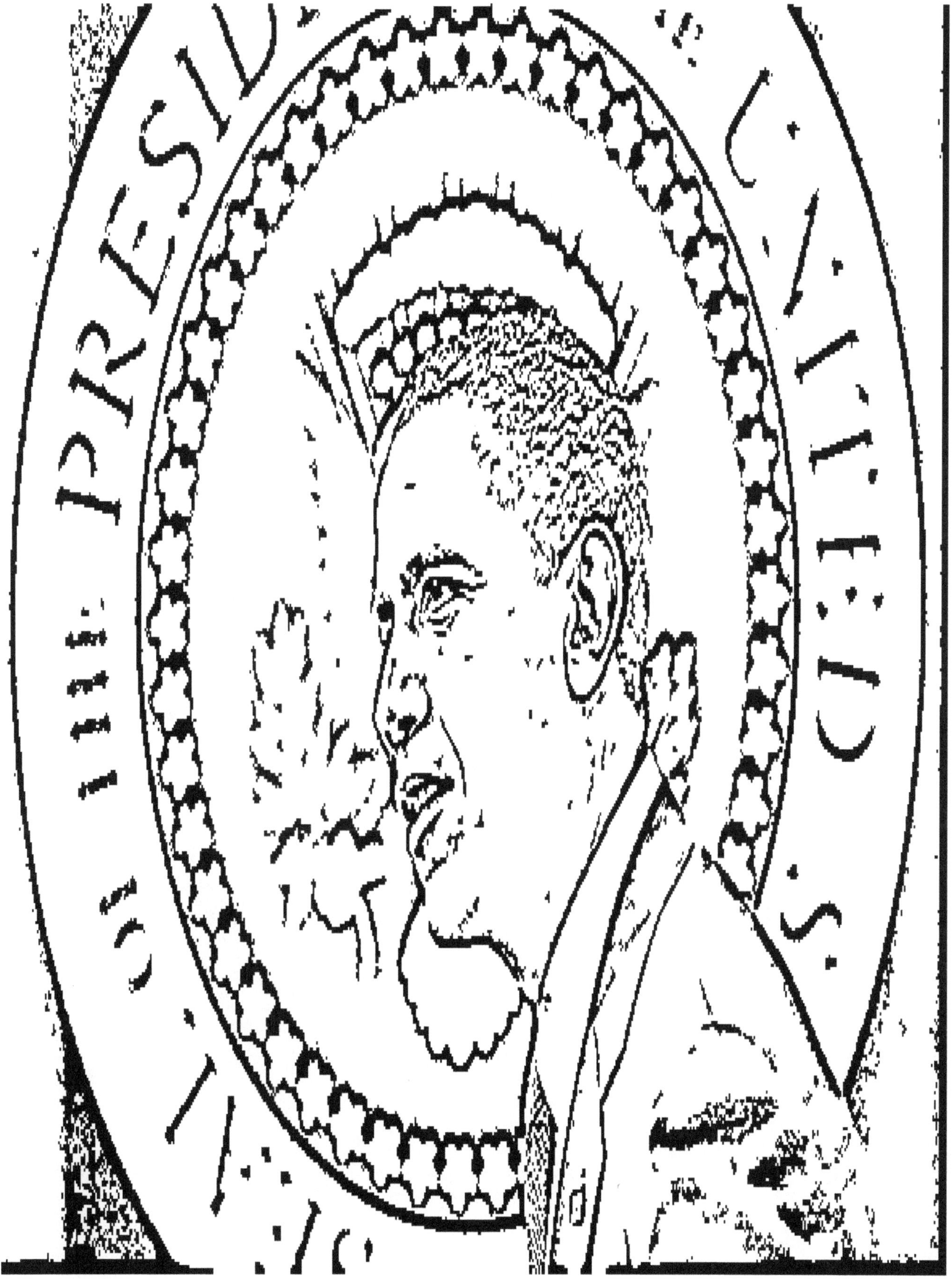

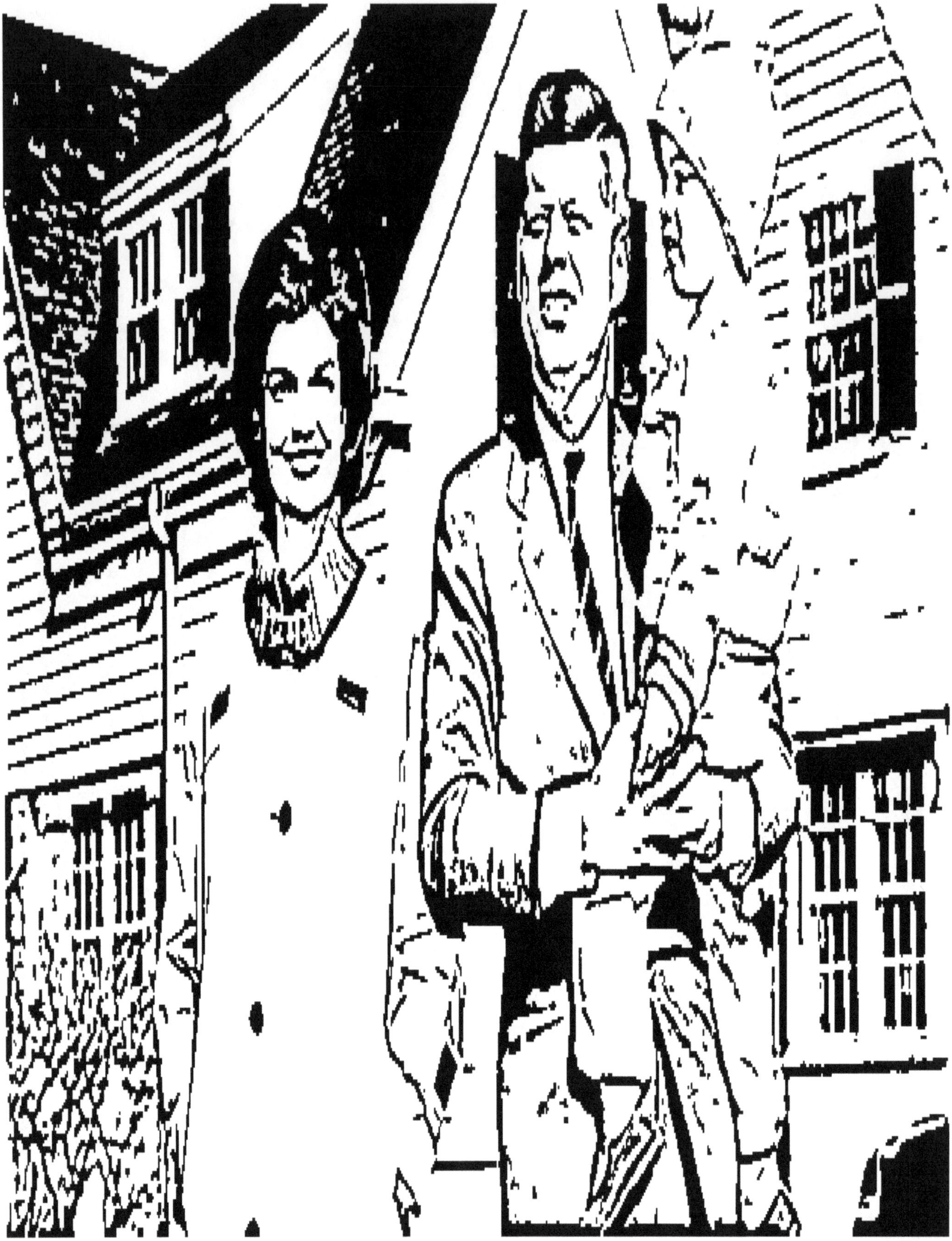

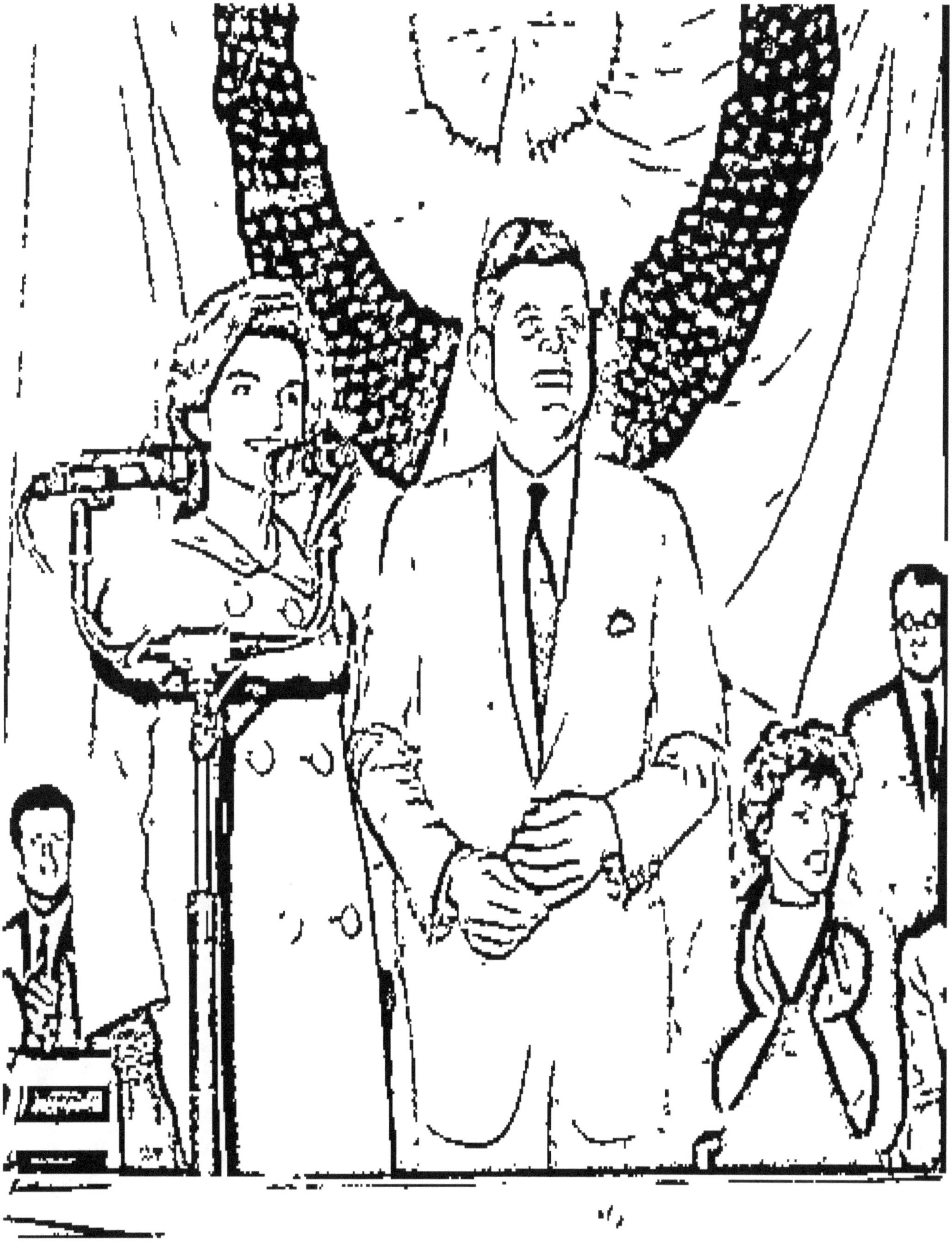

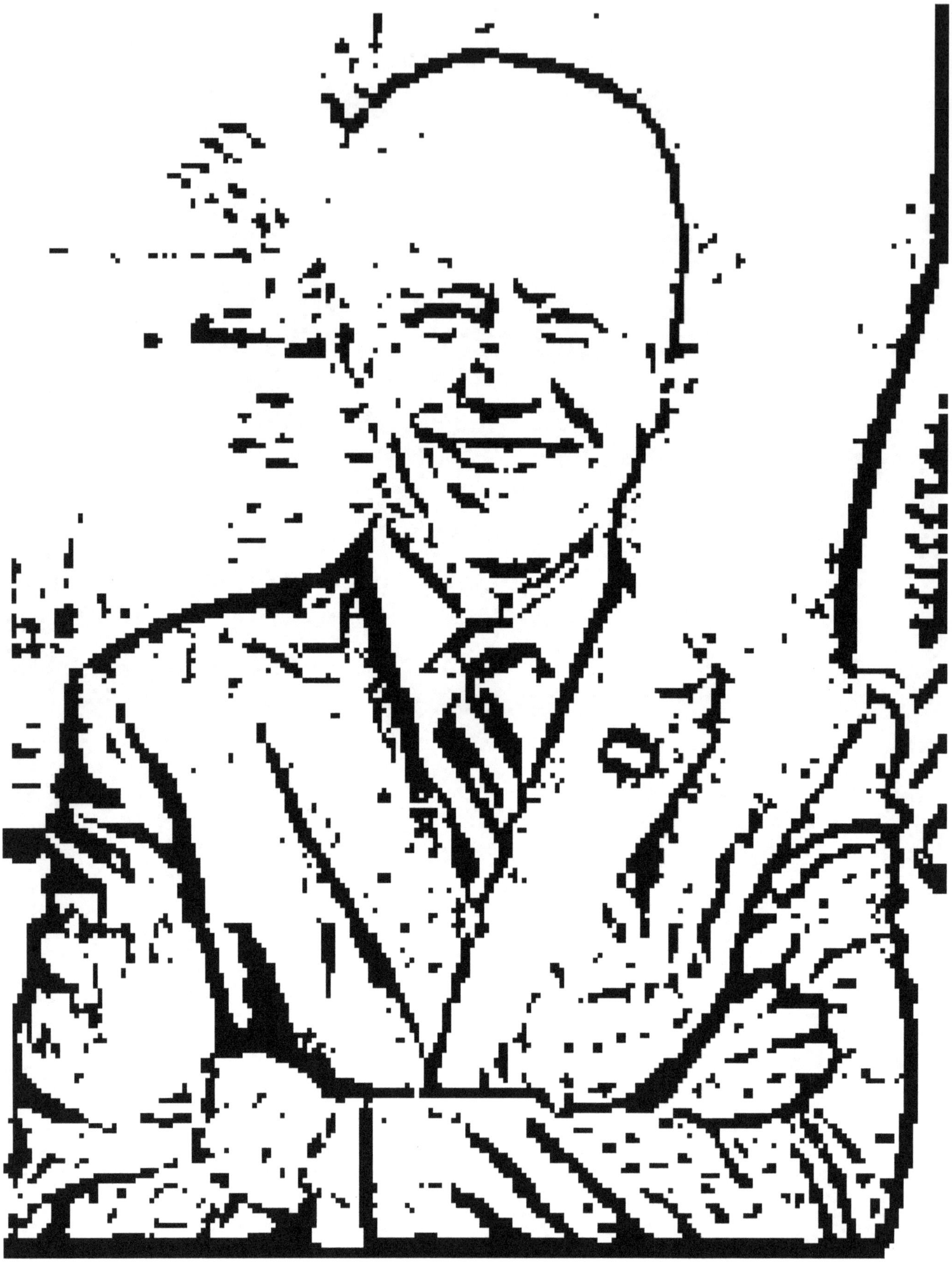

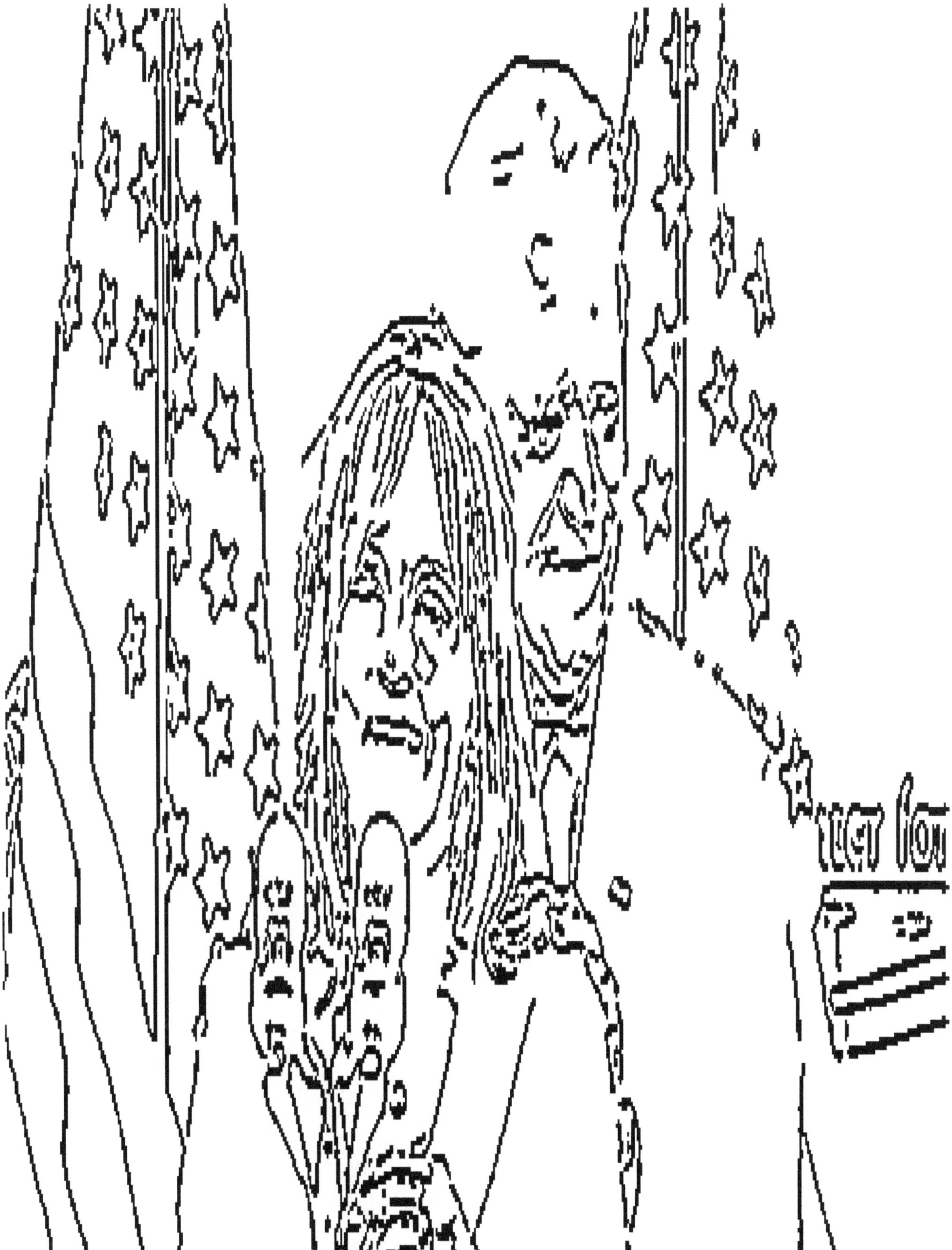

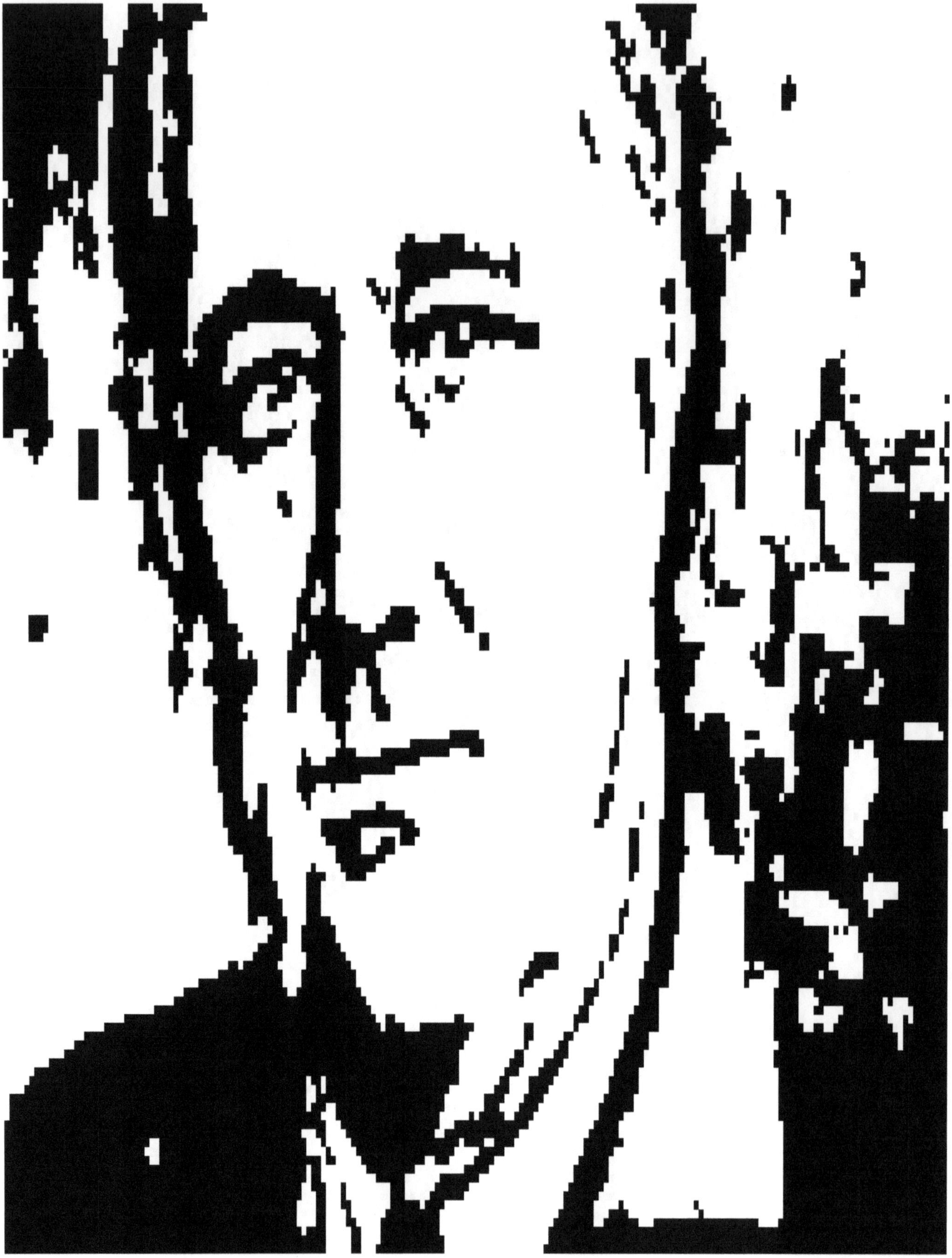

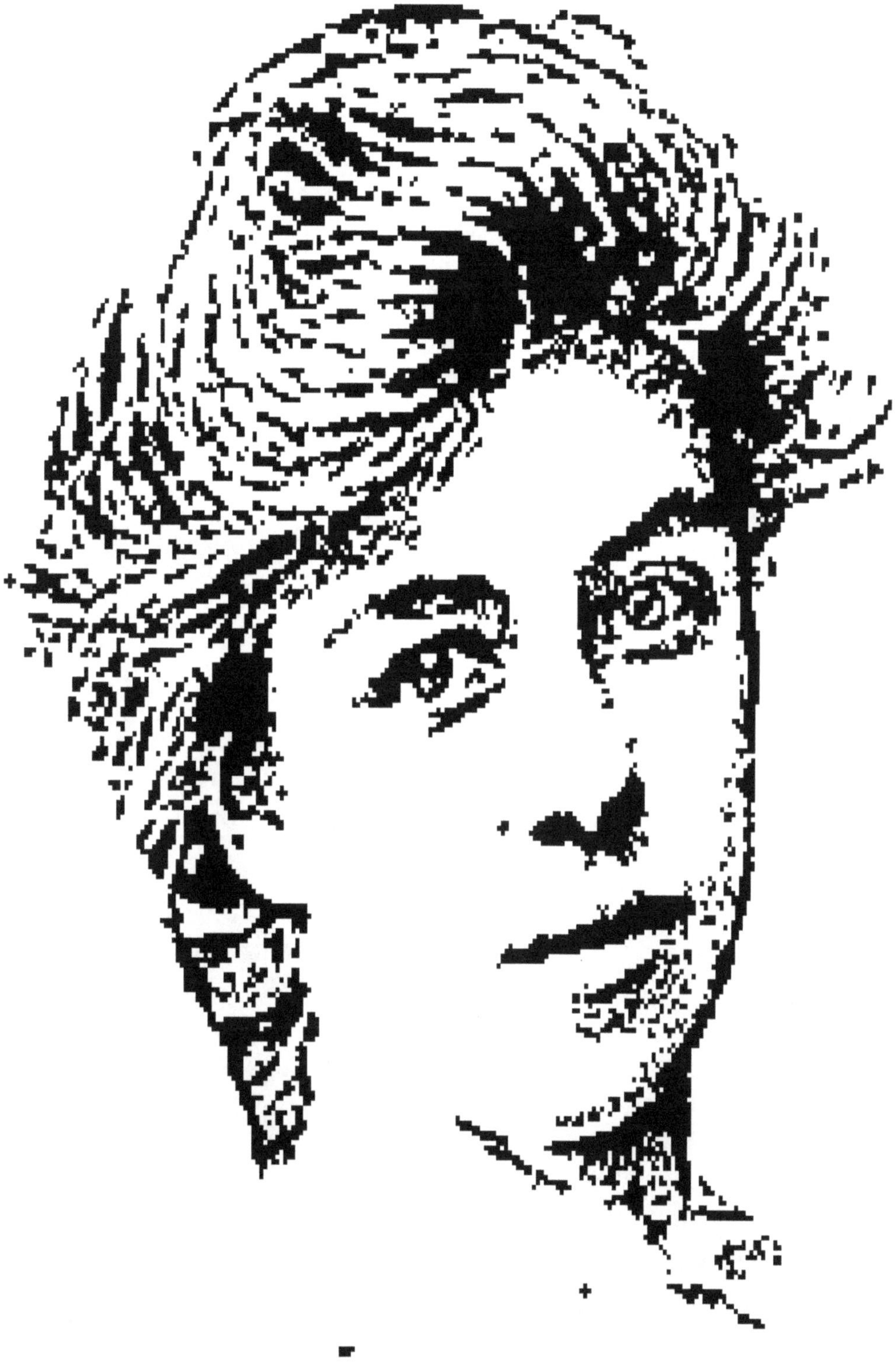

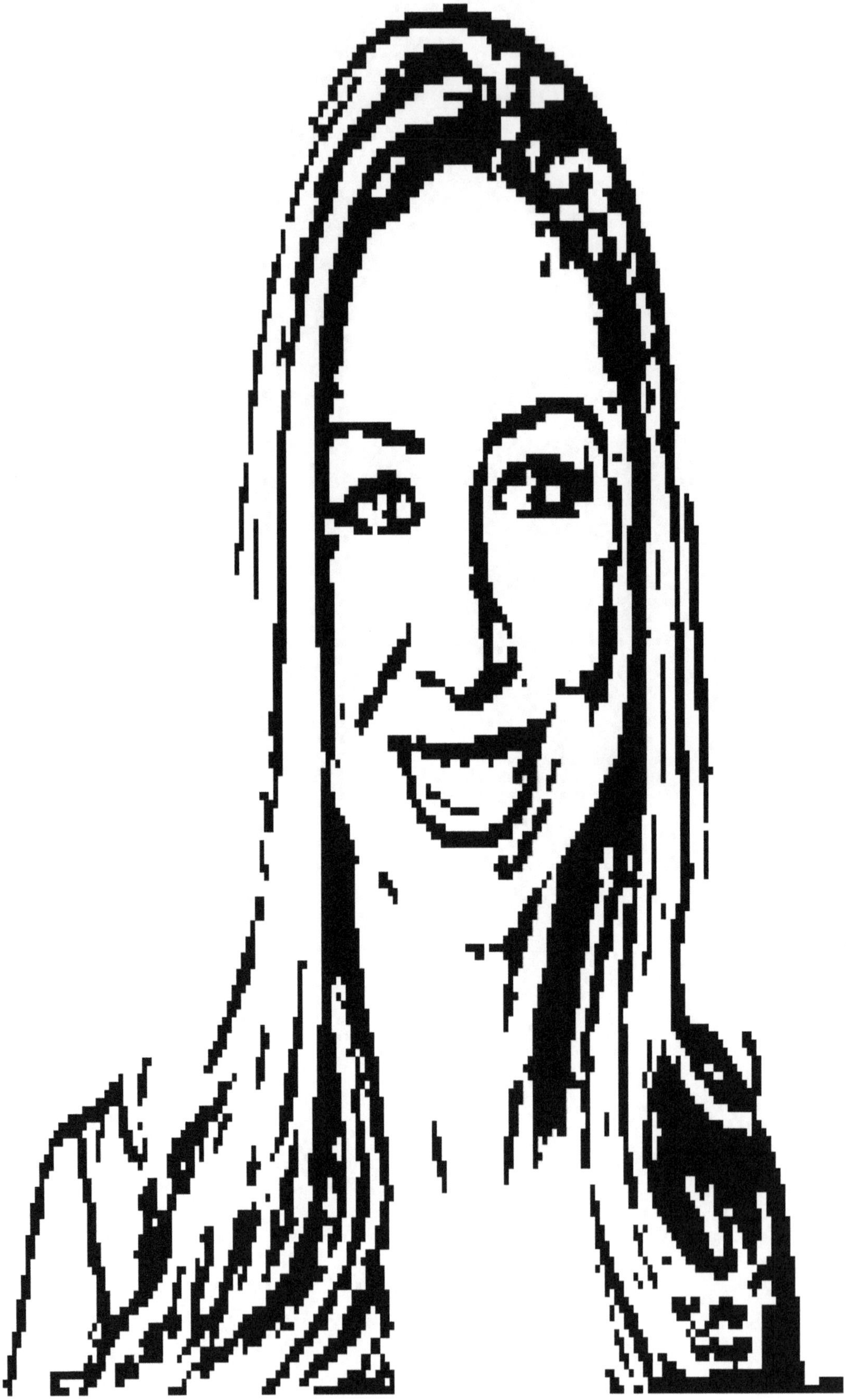

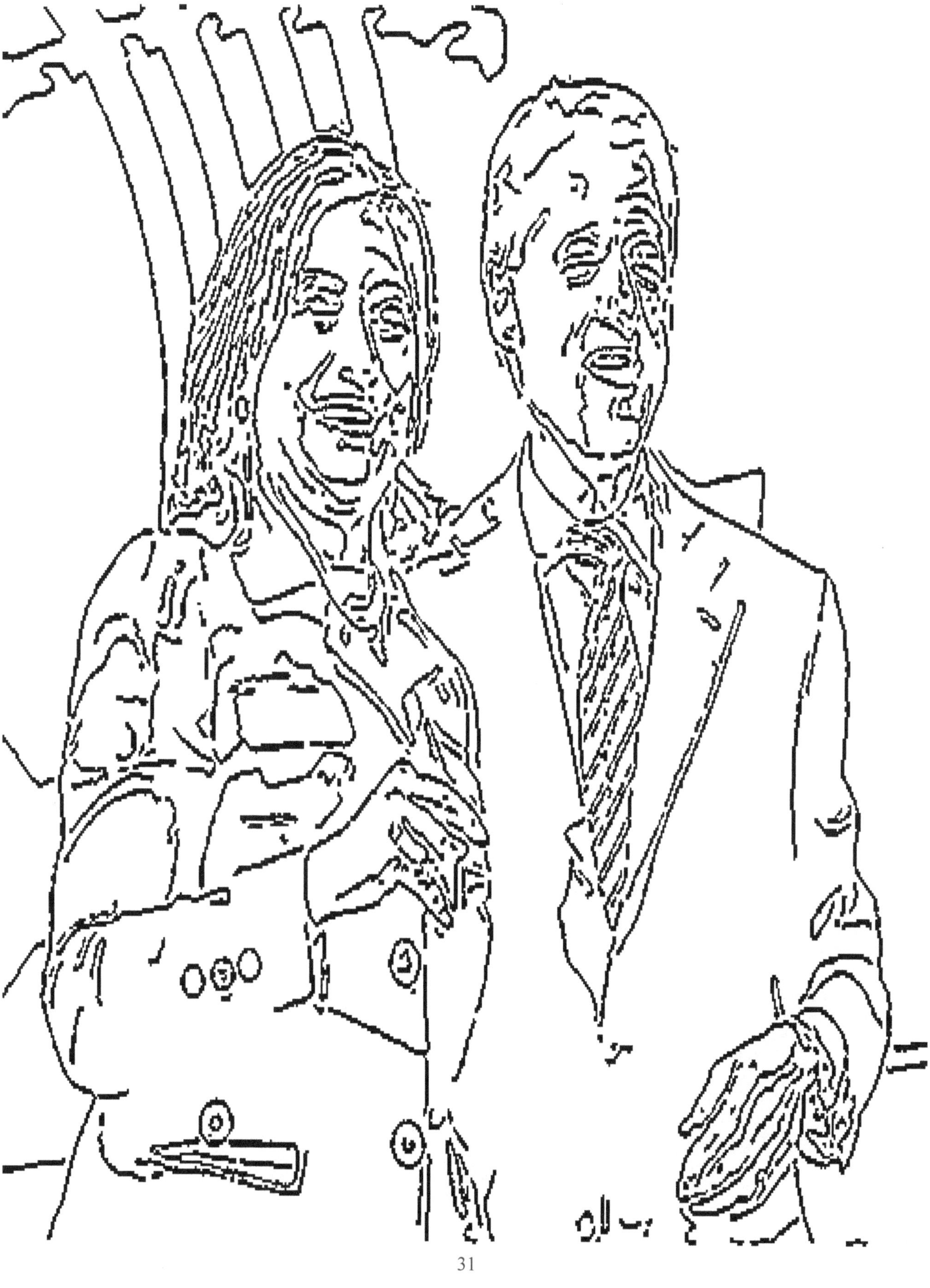

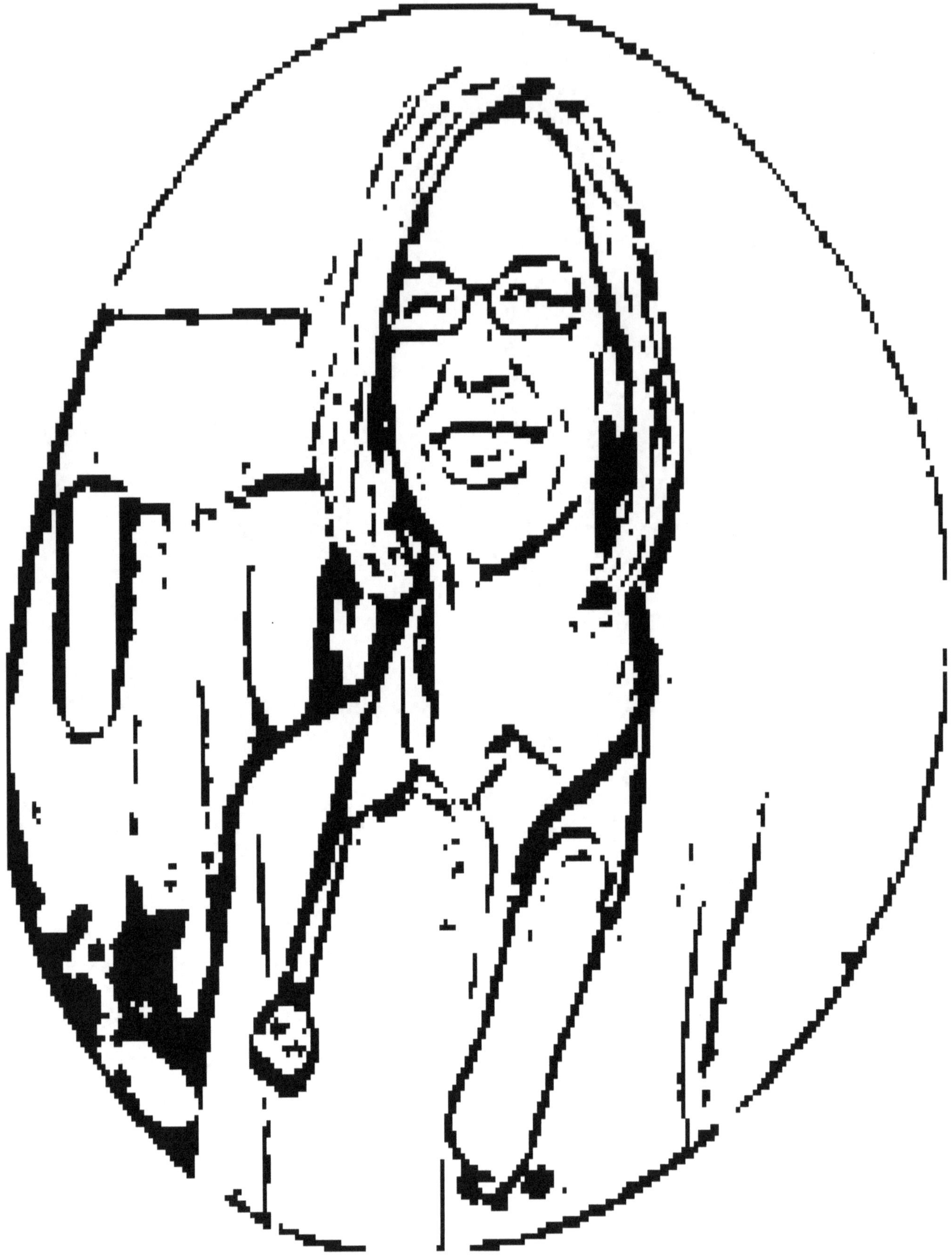

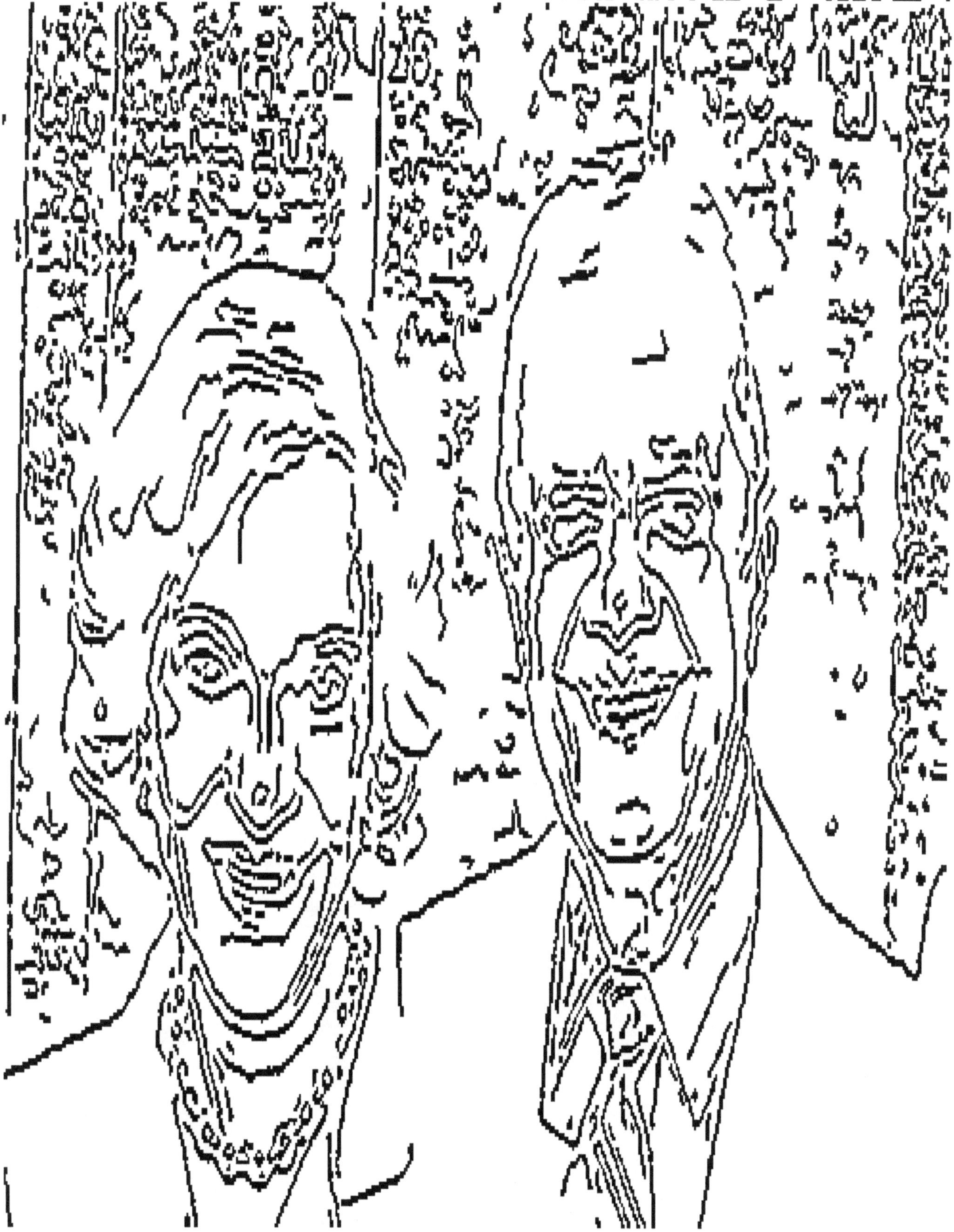

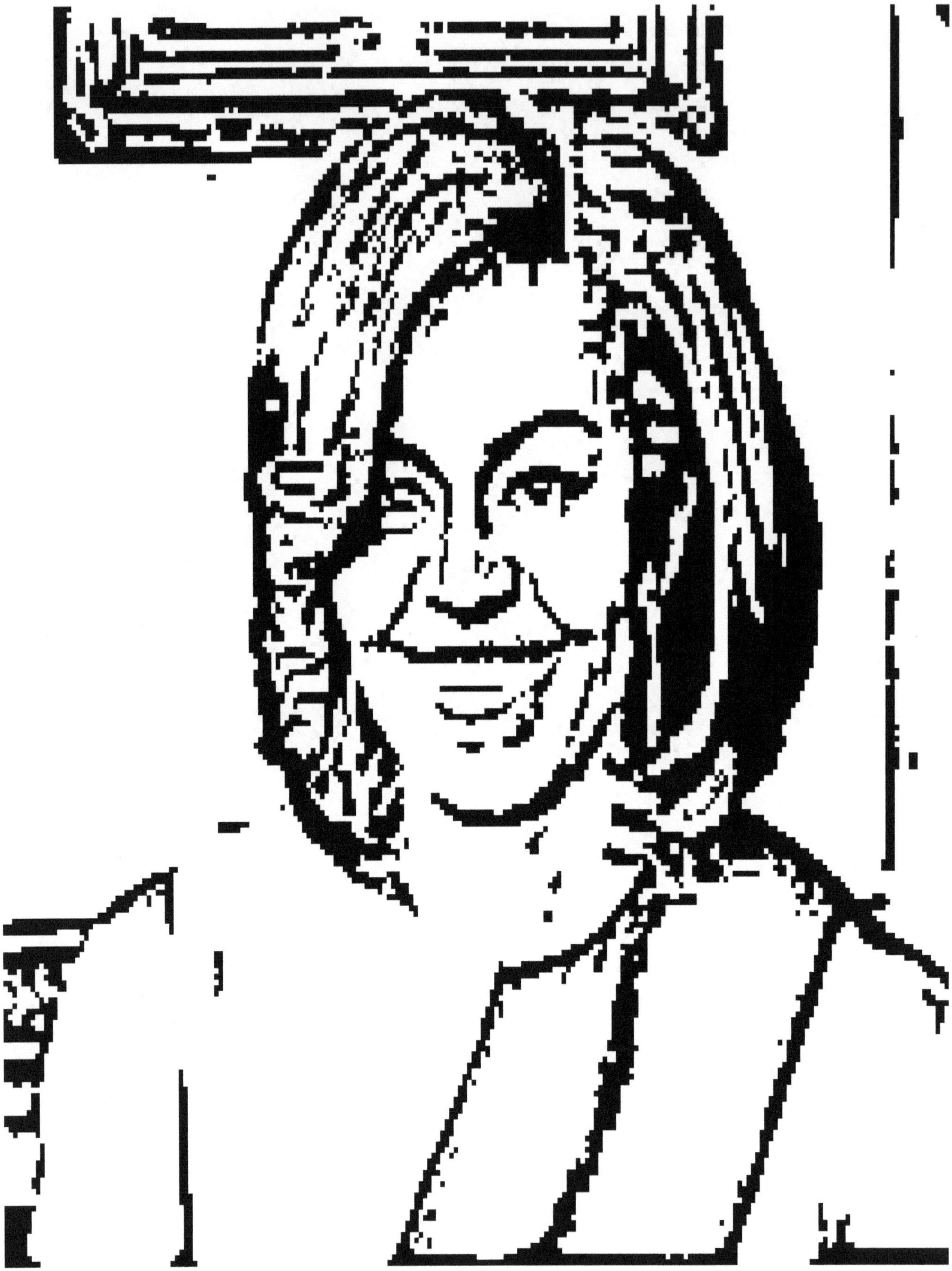

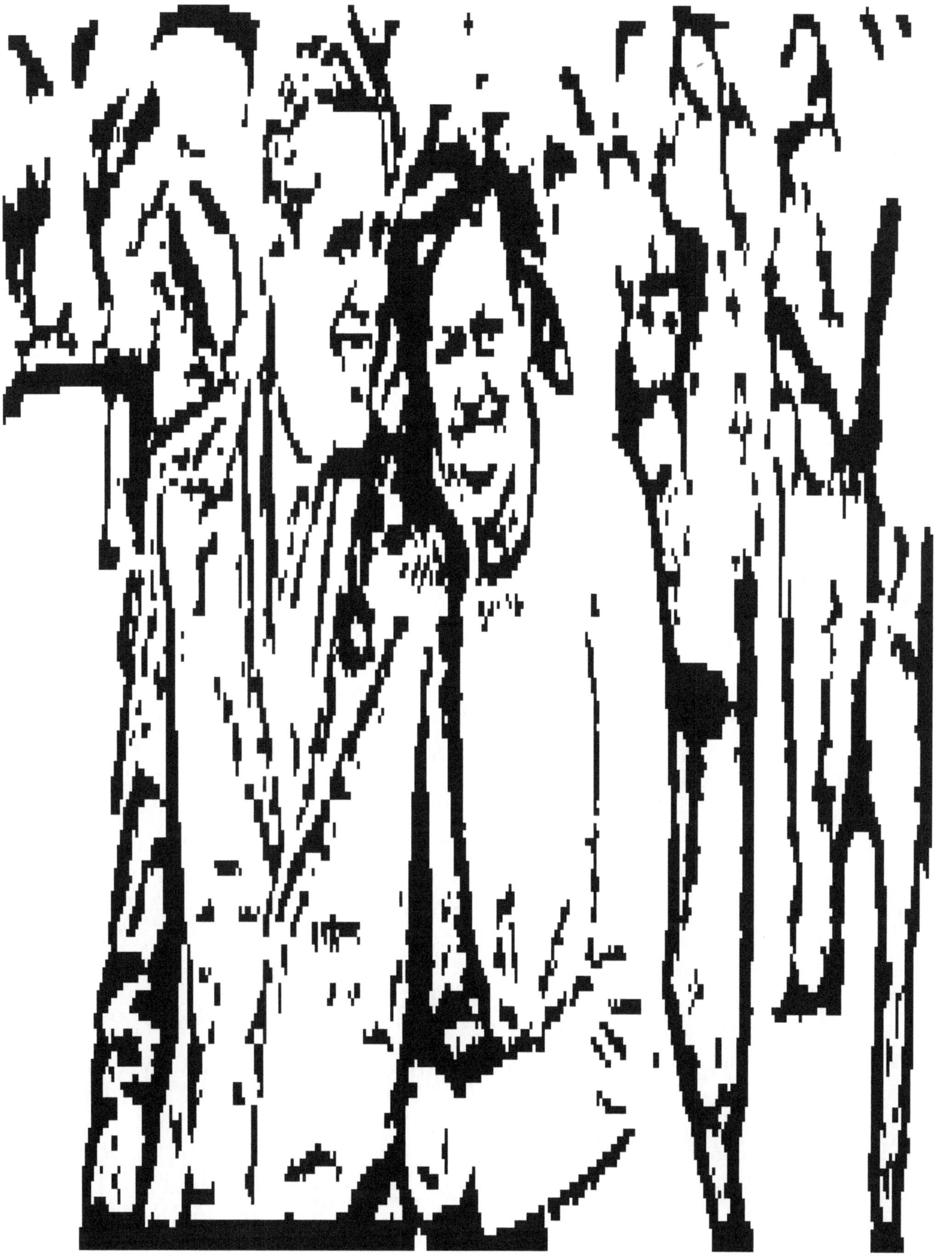

www.ingramcontent.com/pod-product-compliance
Lightning Source LLC
Chambersburg PA
CBHW050908180526
45159CB00007B/2834
9781523875511